BOOK OF WORDS

Book of Words
Doug Rucker
Layout by Helane Freeman

Doug Rucker
Vilimapubco
Malibu, CA
ruckerdoug@gmail.com

Printed in the United States of America

Library of Congress Control Number: 2016915720

ISBN 978-0-9968060-5-3

First Edition
10 9 8 7 6 5 4 3 2 1

CONTENTS

FOREWORD

In 1991, I struggled to produce my first book, one of poetry, with seven chapter endings in prose, about how my poems reflected mental processes during my divorce. It was called <u>Personal Journey</u>.

Over the following thirteen years. I cartooned and created thirteen perfect-bound comedy books and made 50 copies of each and gave them to friends and relatives. Then, in 1998 and 2001, I wrote two volumes of my autobiography, <u>Early Stories</u> and <u>Groundwork</u>. In 2003, I decided to put my entire poetic works in one volume for easy reference and titled the book <u>Moving Through</u>. In 2005, I produced volume three of my autobiography called <u>Growing Edge</u>.

I have written <u>Book of Words</u> to put certain essays into a book for a personal reference. They were written during moments between architectural works, family gatherings and writing other books. The fun of writing is in taking an objective look at what's been going on as time goes by. If the essays continue to give me something back, I count them as worth saving and they become motivation for another try. If the essays don't hold up I file them away. In <u>Book of Words,</u> I have selected written material I want to remember. They are examples of my thoughts at various times over a period of 30 years, and I have assembled them easily if not intelligently. Actually, they're assembled arbitrarily. Certain essays in a book can't be far away. Somewhere between these two covers, I suspect.   *Doug*

BOOK OF WORDS

WRITERS AND READERS

I must confess I am not a writer. I am a person! Writers are special and think deep thoughts and let them flow on paper for us to read, but what about us persons who have not had the time or inclination to study writing? Haven't we rights, too? As the owner of a piano claims the right to strike the keys even though listeners may not call it music, I claim the right to write.

We persons have thoughts too, and why not set them down? 'Course, soon as you set them down, some people will begin calling you a writer, especially if they read what you wrote or see you writing.

Imagine a person coming upon another who is writing, then telling a friend in a confidential tone, *"Yeah! I came down the hall and saw him through the glass door. He was writing things down on paper."*

Shocked, the second would exclaim, *"What is he, a <u>writer</u>?"*

To examine writers for a moment, writers are always persons. Animals, birds, fish and reptiles can't write, let alone plants and rocks. They can't hold a pen in their paw and they can't spell worth a ding-dang. They don't understand language, either, at least ours. *(Perhaps there is understanding between members of their own kind, but very few hieroglyphics or strange markings have been found that could be interpreted as animal writing.)* Animals are <u>not</u> writers.

Animals communicate by looks and gestures. Ever see a dog give you a look and you wondered what he thought of you? Or they may let you know they want to go out by jumping up and down, yipping and barking back and forth from you to the door. Or, if they want to eat, they may point to their mouth with their paw and then to their bowl and look at you with anxious eyes. Or they may want you to feel guilty, perhaps by slinking quietly into a corner and curling up, mournful and alone. We understand them, but not by written words. It is important to establish what is <u>not</u> a writer. Dogs are not writers. *(Buildings and trees are not writers either.)*

People, only, are writers. Male or female, tall or short, fat or thin, foreign or domestic, they are the only species that show even the slightest possibility of becoming writers. They have a language and they can spell. They like to learn new things by thinking and reading. They observe and look inward. They have curiosity and hopes and fears and joys. They feel playful or frustrated or delighted or harried or curious or are loving or bothered or concerned or upset, or are in any one of an infinite number of passions and emotions. These are the essential qualities of a writer. They can only be <u>people</u>!

Yes, people are writers! Now what do you call a person who lives, has experiences, goes through all the trials, hilarities, fears, traumas and contentment's of everyday life, but never puts them down on paper? He or she might be a lot of wonderful things, but one thing he or she most definitely would <u>not</u> be, would be a writer. In order for a person to be a writer, he or she has to set words down on paper for his or her own enjoyment and for others to read. And that's the way it is! OK?

Now a word about perception: All writers have a need to be perceived. Otherwise, why would they write? And whom do they write for? Why readers, of course! In our society lots of people can read. They read the bus schedule. They read *"Men"* and *"Women"* signs on public bathroom doors. They read the directions on medication bottles, but many are not the kind of reader necessary to a writer. A writer doesn't care about this kind of reader. He wants his readers to perceive his inner soul, or groove on his personal uniqueness, or understand his personal point of view. Where does he find these kinds of readers? Let me tell you. They are rare!

A perceiving reader is always like the writer who would be perceived. Both are in search of solutions within the realm of their own personal ignorance

(The personal ignorance realm is that vast area of the brain that has <u>no</u> knowledge.)

Within that vast realm lie the greatest adventures. So writers write to explore the vast realm of their own ignorance and readers read and explore it with him to do the same and have their own adventures in their own vast realm. Writers and readers, discovering and growing, have the greatest adventures.

MOTIVATION

*I*t has been one of my philosophies that if anyone writes a jumble of words until they have reached the amount to fill a book, then the reader, if any, would know more than he might care to know about the writer.

What would the writer learn? He might learn about himself. Or he might not. It depends on whether he is motivated to learn about himself or not.

What is it about motivation? Motivation seems to be the hardest thing to come by. It's difficult to be motivated. *Motivation is more important than what is produced.* If one is motivated, one will produce anything, but whether or not it will be worthwhile needs appraising. I might be motivated to buy an ice cream cone. A really big one! A triple-decker, rocky road with chocolate sauce, ground nuts, whipped cream and a cherry on top!

But still, what motivates my desire for a cone? Hunger of course. Not <u>real</u> hunger, but a <u>sort-of</u> hunger. Not hunger like the need for relief in the depressed cities of Bangladesh, but more a hunger of the rich. I'm not sure hunger is the proper word. Perhaps, *wimpy-little-kinda-wanna-sorta-hankerin'-for-a-little-extra,* might be the proper word – or words. I might want a cherry pie to go, but now I'm far from discussing real hunger or serious motivation.

Einstein was motivated to discover E=MC^2. I don't think I will discover anything like E=MC^2, particularly since I got a D in Physics. I would like to be deeply motivated to do <u>something!</u>

What motivated me to do writing right now? I was reading some old poetry I'd written 20 years ago and questioning how I could have written such weird stuff with lines having no relationship, one to the other.

"Big tree, buried roots, tangled in ground," then, *"little fish, troubled eye, deep water"* and, *"Mary had a little lamb whose fleece was white as snow and everywhere that Mary went the lamb was sure to go."* But of course you know that little verse. And so ends my motivation story! Others could have said more. I wish I had.

TERRIBLE WORDS

*H*ow many words in a 250 page book is the question today. I remove myself to count the words on a page in a book. *Pause.* There are approximately 250 words per page per relatively average book, which, times 250 pages, equals 62,500 words.

Protégé: "I like lots of illustrations."

Roy: "I could have guessed a man of your caliber would like illustrations best. But what is it in the above paragraphs? *Stream of consciousness*, dear reader. Not of James Joyce's worthiness, perhaps, but of a similar genre. *Stream of consciousness* is a process of thinking and visualizing during life as a *process* – as cheese is processed. And so, life, books, words, and blocks of cheese, being of the same genre, are processed."

Protégé: "What?"

Roy: "Nothing."

Protégé: "What shall we do now, Master Le Roy?"

Roy: "We shall write a 250 page book containing 62,500 words."

Protégé: "And what shall the words be, Master Le Roy?"

Roy: "Consecutive! And, of the process genre."

Protégé: "What does genre mean, Master?"

Roy: "A kind or type – as in literature."

Protégé: "Thank you, Master. Is it time for an illustration?"

Roy: "No! Of course not! It's time to play Terrible Words!"

Protégé: "What is Terrible Words, Master?"

Roy: "Terrible Words is a game involving words you and I probably never heard of, like the word *'rutilant,'* for instance."

Protégé: "What does rutilant mean, Master Le Roy?"

Roy: "Rutilant means to have a reddish glow, glowing, gleaming or glittering."

Protégé: "Like W. C. Fields nose?"

Roy: "Something like that. Take the word *'lobscouse.'* Few people know *lobscouse* is a sailor's stew of meat, vegetables and hardtack."

Protégé: "Say, this is fun. What other Terrible Words do you know, Master?"

Roy: "How about the word 'superheterodyne?'"

Protégé "What does that mean, Master Le Roy?"

Roy: "Superheterodyne is a designation of a form of radio reception in which part of the amplification prior to demodulation is carried out at an intermediate, supersonic frequency produced by beating the frequency of the received carrier waves with that of locally-generated oscillation."

Protégé: "Whooooeeee! You sure are smart, Master Le Roy. That's sure a Terrible Word all right. Right on! I'm tired of this game now. Where'd you learn stuff like that, anyhow?"

Roy: "I didn't learn it, I just copied it out of the dictionary."

ETERNITY

*I*t is my habit to go jog-walking in the morning five or six days a week before I begin the day's work. I went this morning, worked up a sweat, thought about things that needed thinking about and finished in the leisurely time of 48 minutes and 35 seconds. Then I did a few arm exercises, bracing my arms against a railing and doing 30 inclined push-ups. Afterwards, I took 15 pound weights in each hand and curled them 60 times, swinging them overhead every five curls. When I finished, my arms and chest were pumped up and I felt big, powerful and capable.

But while I was doing the curls, I noticed a little black dot moving slowly and quietly across the concrete slab. It was a little larger than a speck, and moved only four to six inches during my exercising. I wondered what kind of creature was way down there while I was way up here swinging my arms. What kind of life did it lead? It wasn't an ant or fly or spider. Just a tiny black dot moving hesitantly but steadily in what seemed a totally arbitrary direction. Was it looking for food? Was it taking a little walk? Did it really have any idea why in heaven's name it found itself on my concrete slab making its trip to nowhere while I exercised? Slowly it passed a hairline crack then made its laborious way around a little piece of dirt.

When I finished my curling and arm lifts I had to have a better look at this living dot, so I leaned way down from my great height and put my hands on my knees, and my nose within a foot of the living thing, and discovered it was a beetle with an oblong shell and an abundance of almost-invisible feet. Its feelers projected a millimeter in front, wavering slightly as the beetle moved in its timeless way. The bug was as alert as any bug can be and apparently knew where it was going, taking great care to maneuver perfectly on his journey.

I thought about smashing him to a pulp – a spot on the pavement – no big deal. I had just finished reading a history of the 14th century about the chivalry of knights galloping swiftly to battle in full armor astride magnificent horses with lances and swords and bludgeons. I thought of the cheapness of life in those times, and had read about never-ending wars, backbreaking taxes and tortuous punishments during the era of the black plague. From the bug's standpoint, I might have been an armored knight on a leaping horse or a seasoned warrior with a thirst for blood. If I crushed him, in the larger scheme of things, what difference would it make? Then I thought if I was crushed by a real knight, what difference would that make? If we, the bug and I, were each crushed, in the larger scheme of things, it would make no difference.

As I watched him move, I caught a glimpse of eternity.

This harmless creature existed right in front of me not knowing how he got into this world, yet doing something nature carefully designed him to do; living and making decisions for reasons completely unknown to him. And here I was, existing and making my way through the world, with reasons just as completely foreign to me; going about my business as nature designed me to do. I wasn't any more aware of why I was in this world than he. The beetle and I were the same. It was our job to do the things nature had designed us to do. So I decided to be here and do what I was designed to do, including jog-walking, exercising, experiencing laughter and sadness, catching glimpses of eternity and having all the other human strengths and frailties. Relative to his world, the beetle was doing the same. I love the bug.

A WELL THOUGHT-OUT BOOK

*I*f one were to write a book like I'm doing right now, one might ask what kind of a book to write? How might the end product look? What would be the characteristics of a well thought-out book? The following things come to mind.

A carefully thought-out book would have something interesting to say. This would depend, of course, on the capabilities of the writer, and since I'm the writer and my capabilities are what they are, the content of the book will be what it will be. I shall do my best to compose according to my premise: <u>off the top of my head.</u>

A carefully thought-out book would be nice to feel and attractive to look at. It should inspire pride of ownership. One should be able to say, inwardly, *"This book is mine. I want to keep it. It has things in it that absorb me. It makes me feel good to have this book. I identify with things I find in it. It expresses a lot of my own viewpoint. The author and I see things similarly and he/she says things I would say, were I not busy with my life."*

Or he might disagree with, but respect the author's viewpoint, and like the book because it gives him a chance to test his own beliefs and experiences against those of the writer. A book worth keeping, one cherished and kept close when others have been misplaced, is one that, like a friend, is supportive of the reader's sense of worth. It is my opinion that if a writer can touch the reader's sense of personal worthiness, he will have written a book that stays in collections.

To enhance the content, the pages should be neat and clean and of appropriate material. The format should be clear, pleasing to look at, and easy to follow, clarity being a major asset to a well thought-out book. Who would bother with a book that's tedious to follow? I'd throw it down in disgust! And uniqueness? A book lacking in uniqueness is destined for obscurity. A carefully planned book will be one-of-a-kind, charismatic, and special in its feel, its look and content.

A good book should speak personally to the reader in a refreshingly new way. Its point of view should be unique to its subject matter and shed a different light, be another facet, show another side. The content can express ideas or imagery, but must be clearly set forth. This can be achieved by leaving wide, white margins, having few, but clearly delineated paragraphs, or text interspersed with drawings or photographs pertaining to its subject matter.

The content must be carefully written or drawn; all extraneous words left out, cast away, rejected. *(This calls for great decisive powers.)* All necessary words must be in their appropriate places. Words, being the building blocks of an idea or image, must be strong, lest as weak bricks comprise a weak wall, so the whole thought becomes less clear and is compromised. Leave that which can be left out, out. Include only those building block words that strengthen the thought, idea, description, concept, proposal, story line, argument, episode, poem, verbal arrangement, or that idea or image that is to be conveyed. For an average book conveys a point of view and a well thought-out book conveys it better.

Books are a method of communication, one person to another on a one-to-one basis. They are better than television or conversation in that the reader, who is the willing participant, can review the thought or idea he has just read about as many times as he wishes in order to understand. Books are capable of being studied because they are dimensionally-stable storehouses of information instantly retrievable and don't evaporate into thin air moments after utterance like the spoken word. One can ponder a book as time permits, and a good book will be highly ponderable.

The writer of a good book conveys his personal slant on things directly to the reader who then participates in the communication, silently agreeing or disagreeing, loving, hating, hoping, enjoying, being angry, appalled, disturbed, or delighted or being involved in whatever is precipitated in his mind. In a well thought-out book, a reader will have a unique experience, one he has never experienced before. He will open it with passion and expectancy for he has felt the cover, seen the format, determined its clarity and appearance, and is now anxious to test its unique worth by participating in its content and enjoying a positive, personal, one-on-one adventure.

DEEP, RICH THOUGHTS

*I*t is my purpose today to think deep, rich thoughts. I have just listened to Beethoven's Third Symphony on the radio and it was pretty good. It is obvious to me that he was thinking deep, rich, great, sage-like thoughts when he wrote it, otherwise it wouldn't be charged with such power, brilliance and meaning.

OK! Here I go! I'm going to think a deep, rich, meaningful thought, filled with sage-like power, the likes of which, when it is quoted later on, will be thought to be ... like, they will say, *"Wow! This guy really had it! Like, I mean, you know ... "* Just like I say that now of Beethoven.

Right now, then! I have been inspired by Beethoven to do it! Here goes ... *(time passes) ... (about four minutes)* ... There! I have thought it!

Question: How long does it take to think a great thought? We have no statistics on the matter. There has been no research among the great to ascertain just how long it takes to think a really great thought.

There are lots of points of discussion, though, such as, and you may quote me, *"Sometimes a greater thought is thought in less time than a lesser thought."* This is difficult to prove, however, because there are so many disputes as to which are the greater and which the lesser thoughts.

Also, sometimes people, myself included, think a pretty good thought may take them, let's say, twenty-five minutes, or so, then lie about how fast they did it.

Some great thoughts that I can think of right off the top of my head are that governments should be of the people, for the people, and by the people. I don't mean to get political, but how does this contrast with the thought that the world is round like an orange, not flat like a pancake.

Thoughts like the above are discoveries rather than thoughts. To some, though, they seem like thoughts. You can see how confusing this discussion can get. It has immense complexity. I shall attempt to keep my discussion as simple as possible. For instance, a pure thought, as against the less pure discovery, would be, like ... *"Hey! I just remembered where I put my car keys!"* Now, at first glance this seems like a thought, but upon close examination, it checks out as a memory.

So, we cannot call memories thoughts any more than we can call discoveries thoughts. Which leaves us with the question, what thoughts are deep and rich? And what, then, is pure thought? How long does it take to think a deep, rich thought? Who is the fastest, swiftest, Super-Bowl-champ-thinker of thoughts? Does speed affect quality? These and other questions must be answered if human enlightenment is to continue.

For human enlightenment, then, I have come up with

a scale for thoughts. I call it my one-to-ten scale. The higher the number, the higher the quality. You follow this, I'm sure. Then I use the common watch or *"clock"* to time the thoughts from beginning to end; from the first rarified, silent nuance of an inkling to a full blown, mature, beautifully conceived, deep, rich thought.

I will test it out right now ... *(I'm thinking)* ... *(now I'm getting an inkling)* ... Oh! Woweeee! I've got it! I just got this great thought -- SHORT-RISE SWEAT PANTS! Yes, folks, for those who like the sweat pant legs longer than the crotch rise, I have this new thought ... Like, I have these sweat pants at home? And when I pull them up so the pant crotch fits, the leg bottoms are at my knees and the waistband ties over my head. I have cut holes in the *"long-rise"* section to see out, which is OK for seeing straight ahead, but no good for seeing side-to-side. Short-Rise Sweat Pants is the thought for today.

Think important thoughts, quick! I timed myself for the above at one second and rate myself a *"nine."* How do you rate?

HAPPY BIRTHDAY, DAVE

Birthdays are wonderful! They mark the passage of time. They let you know time is going by and that you are part of that time. Kind of like ... let's say, you are part of the river and you begin flowing at the river source ... actually ... no, wait! Let's say you are just a drop and you mingle with other droplets forming a trickle *(hopefully you are not acid rain)* and you trickle down the slope to the itsy, bitsy, very first little beginning of a sort of tributary rivulet, and you are in the middle of your funny tributary rivulet making your way into a somewhat deeper ... let's say, barranca, where you meet hundreds of other droplets, flowing and in the same direction.

Pretty soon you reach the end of the barranca and are dumped into a bona fide creek and you flow around boulders and through sticks and leaves until you reach a tributary river and you're pickin' up speed and begin to feel the surge and power of all the little droplets around you and you are starting to get high. Your adrenals begins pumping from the top of your kidneys sending waves of *"fight-or-flight"* messages into your body and you are getting just a little giddy and are just trying to hang on to yourself, when you come pouring into a mighty river.

Like being in a main runoff artery, you are swept midstream down ... let's say, like the Mississippi River ... flowing with the current, mainstream. Just picture yourself ... out in the mainstream of the Mississippi River, looking toward shore *(as your own tiny droplet)* ... watching forests and farms go by, ferry boats, docks, cities, clouds, and blue sky above, and sun ... hot ... flowing ... mainstream ... Ah! Where was I? Ah, what was I talking about? I don't know. Anyway, you are a raindrop in the middle of a river ... giddy and about ready to faint with the power of it all ... and you think nothing can be this high ... but, you ain't seen nothin' yet ... because about when you're learning you can handle the mainstream of a mighty river, your drop-particle speeds up, flows around a fan-shaped bunch of piled up silt and pours into the Gulf of Mexico.

Now you're drifting around in the middle of the Gulf of Mexico, bobbing up and down on little waves, maybe 400 miles off the Florida Coast ... and you don't know what's in store for you, but you sense something is going to happen because the sea is heaving in strange rhythms and the air is deathly quiet. You don't know it, but the Florida Early Storm Warning System has just predicted Hurricane Disasterella is about to hit Miami Beach at 4:00 A. M. in the morning. If you woulda known that, you'da stayed in bed, but all you can do now is say ... *"Gulp!"* ... and are just sitting out there in the deathly calm, strange, heaving, water, when ... Pow! Something hits you like a meteor from outer space!

You think to yourself, after all I've been through, running down the grassy slopes, mingling with the raindrops in the barranca, flowing around the rocks in the bona fide creek, pouring into the mighty river and into the great Gulf of Mexico, what else? Pow! Again! It happens to you! Hurricane Disasterella is on you full force. You try to hold your breath and dive so deep under the water the hurricane won't get you, but too late! You are airborne at jet speed: 0 to 200 miles per hour in 1.5 seconds.

What happens next is too indescribable for words. You would have to listen to the final scherzo of Beethoven's Ninth to get the barest suggestion of what it's like to be a drop of water in Hurricane Disasterella, 300 miles off the coast of Florida. Man, your adrenals by this time have shot their wad! You <u>are</u> adrenaline! But then, after a while, you begin to relax. You notice you <u>do</u> have company. There are those other droplets right next to you and they are traveling as fast as you are and so it seems like everything's cool ... you know ... like freeway driving at peak hour when everyone's doing 65 miles an hour. You look out the window and it seems like no one's moving.

And so you begin to relax and just let the wind-energy do the work and you begin to enjoy the ride. You kind of look over at the other drops and sort of ... grin ... and wave. Pretty soon they grin and wave back, and you are astounded because here you are in the middle of Hurricane Disasterella, 200 miles off the coast of Florida, whipped by

200-mile-an-hour winds and you are kind of enjoying the whole experience. You're high and have friends. It is kind of an adventure, and you are thinking it's great and are beginning to get lulled into a weird sense of security when you notice you are falling at a terrifying speed toward earth and you begin to panic again!

When you least expect it and you are praying to God that – SPLAT! You hit a grassy slope. When you come to, you have the sense of deja vu. You've been here before, but you can't remember when. Then you begin to join and mingle and mix with other droplets, and soon you are part of a wet sheet of water flowing down the grass, and the sun comes out and steam begins to rise off the Bayous, and you discover yourself getting smaller and smaller, and a panicky realization comes over you that you may have contracted the dreaded disease called *"evaporation"* – and you begin to yell, *"HELP!"* But your cries get weaker – *"help!"* You're getting smaller and smaller, but it doesn't feel too bad. You begin to have a sense of well-being, a feeling of lifting into the air, a sense of lightness and rightness and OK-ness; a sense of coldness and wetness, the panic is leaving. You and your friends become mist or water vapor and you are swept high in the air and then as the sun sets, to your great joy and delight you've become a RAINBOW! *Happy Birthday, Dave.*

LUCY AND THE CHICKENS
(A story problem)

Lucy Brigum's bedroom is exactly ten feet, six inches from her Dad's 1,100 bird chicken coop. At 2:00 AM one morning, one of the hens leaned against a small pane of glass that fell from its frame and soon a steady stream of chickens were quietly clucking and poking their heads through Lucy's doggy-door flap, entering her room, scratching, walking and hopping all over the place. If they entered at the rate of 200 chickens per hour, and half were on her bed, how many chickens did Lucy see on her covers when she awoke at 6:00 AM?

A) How many feet were there if one-quarter of the chickens had only one leg?

B) How many toes?

PROTÉGÉ

I have a young person that visits me who wants to become an architect. *(I am an experienced architect.)* He shows me his recent drawings and I comment on them. I consider myself his mentor, of sorts.

I like him. He's 19 years of age and has all the hopes, dreams, fears and ambivalences of his age and the age in which we live. I told him to strike the words *should and ought* from his vocabulary and substitute the words *I will* and *I won't*.

I told him if he got past *duty* and *desire*, he'd be all right. Of course, I knew I was talking to myself. The best teachers are those desperate to teach subjects they love. I told him to *go from his living spirit directly to his personal expression, as a tree unfolds towards the sky*.

He looked at me with shining eyes, little beads of perspiration dotting his forehead. *(Was he on dope?)* I asked myself, and went on. *"Before you are anything, doctor, lawyer, clerk, architect, you must first be yourself. You must oust the struggles within; those internal conflicts, that, like the tapeworm, suck vital juices leaving only dregs of energy for action. You must reach inward, grab the demon, the conflict, by the tail and yank him out, and when you have him wriggling and dripping on the table; you must stifle your scream, and breathe force into yourself and examine him carefully."*

A droplet of sweat rolled off my friend's chin, spotting the front of his shirt. *(Was it time for him to go?)* I asked myself, and then continued my advice. *"I said you must be father to the frightened child within; join in his feelings, be with him in his terrible fears, sympathize in his ugliness and understand his impossible dilemma."* (He must be on <u>something,</u> I thought, *perhaps cocaine. He's not yet twenty. This philosophy is too heavy for him.*)

"YANK THE SHOULDS AND OUGHTS FROM THE BOWELS OF YOUR SOUL AND PLACE, INSTEAD, THE NEW ORDER – DESIRE! Go with the relief, as Viscott would say, and you'll discover nothing less than fulfillment of personal self."

I think to myself, *(Am I getting through? Why does he not say anything? Does he think I'm a fool? Is that a silly grin or is that the normal shape of his face? Am I being too open with him? Does he understand a word I've been saying?)*

"DROP THE CROSS OF SELF DENIAL! (From a Joan Baez song) Affirm yourself and do ONE THING for yourself, alone, each day. Strike the word DUTY from your mind. Fight and die in Vietnam? Wrong!"

My young person, for whom I have great caring, slumps in his chair and will speak, *"When did <u>you</u> find eternal happiness?"*

I am shocked! *"Why ... ah ... last year,"* I responded.

"You mean it took you fifty-seven years?" My friend slightly straightened his chair, his forehead hardly damp.

"Well, I found it eventually." I seated myself more firmly in my chair, elbows on table, and touched my fingertips, feeling defended.

"That's discouraging."

I'm thinking, *(Oh, no. I've discouraged him. Not what I meant to do. I've hit him with too much too fast. He'll never remember it all. Perhaps I should write him a list of my beliefs so he can copy them down and learn how to be ME! Did I say that?)* But, I continue, anyway, *"Find yourself! Then, with yourself, you can be and do anything you'd like. Do not NAIL PLYWOOD OVER THE HOLE OF YOUR LAST ESCAPE, but rather, strip the plywood, grab the edges and hurl it to the ground while climbing forcefully from the restrictions of your personal box!"*

"R-R-R-RIP THE SELF-MADE PRISON, YOUR SHOULDS AND OUGHTS to the ground and trample it ASUNDER, exclaiming to the world at large, I'M ME! I'M ME!"

(Now, where'd he go?)

NORTH POLE

*Y*esterday morning I woke up thinking about the North Pole. I visualized it as a cylindrical red and white striped barber pole about 10 inches in diameter and 10 feet high, marking the exact geographical top of the world; the place from which all directions are South – sort of downhill.

I know it's ridiculous to think a red and white striped barber pole marks the North Pole, but then, what is it marked by? It is inconceivable that all humanity could resist the urge to plunge some kind of marker into such a crucial spot. I suppose it could be marked by a plain old surveyor's stake.

My surveyor friend, Mario, always marks the corners of property with a 2x2 pointed redwood stake that he drives in the ground with a sledgehammer about a foot, leaving the top showing only an inch or so. Then he refines his measurements by driving a nail into the end-grain marking the exact corner – and I mean EXACT! He uses a plumb bob and everything. 'Course, that seems kind of puny, to mark something as important as the North Pole with just a 2x2 stake with a nail in it, even if it IS really accurate.

In the first place, snow would probably cover the stake

the first night and nobody could find it. Or, if the stake were driven into ice, then, if the ice melted, the stake would fall over and maybe a sled dog, a husky, would pick it up in his mouth, then take it to his Eskimo master and want to play fetch. Then his master would say *"Hey! This looks like the surveyor's stake of the North Pole!"* He'd cuff the dog's ears and march back to the North Pole to see if he could find the hole it came out of and try to put it back. But we both know he wouldn't put it back as accurately as Mario, or some other surveyor set it. Some people might come to the North Pole, look at the stake and think, *"That's IT!"* But it might be off a couple of inches. How could we trust it?

Now logically, scientists who use satellites, electronics and lasers as tools for precise measurements probably know the exact location of the North Pole and I feel certain somebody knows the exact position of the North Pole at least in theory. And as far as I know, the Pole may already be marked physically in some way. But if it isn't, then I think it should be marked if only so explorers can be sure they got there.

'Course, if different countries sent their surveyors out to mark the Pole, they would probably disagree a little bit. America would mark it here with a stars-and-stripes flag. Russia would mark it there claiming it with a tricolor flag of white, blue and red. Britain and France would mark it five feet this way or nine feet that way with their national flags. All the lesser countries would probably take a stab at it just for the practice and peg it here or there claiming to be *"right on."* And I can see about a half-acre of little flags marking the exact position of the North Pole and each country claiming it's right.

It concerns me, too, for it seems the exact location of the North Pole should be the ultimately perfect benchmark upon which to base the map of the world and if it's off, well ...

OMNIPOTENCE AND THE FLY

I saw the fly against my bathroom screen looking out. I had to leave, so I closed the sliding glass window to secure the room, trapping the fly outside between the screen and the window. I hated that. The fly could only move in two dimensions, up, down, left, right, but not back and forth. He had lost all angular flying off into the third dimension — into that thick, rich, three-dimensional air he was designed to use so efficiently.

What a crime, I rationalized. Oh, well. There are lots of flies that are totally free; flies that can go anywhere, do anything, and be anything a fly can be. So what if the world has one fly that can move only in two dimensions. But then, I thought, that's not all. The fly was trapped outside the glass, but inside the screen, subject to all weather changes, damp, cold, moist, night wind, rain, dust, heat or whatever was happening out there.

But flies are pretty tough; good survivors. He can last out there, I reasoned ... what a life, though! What about food? He can't pursue food? No juicy trash heaps to feast on. No empty cartons with bits of spoiling yogurt clinging, no smelly, empty old pickle jars to light upon, no banana peels to explore.

What do flies eat? How do flies eat? Perhaps they're not built for eating, only propagating – questions I'm too lazy to look up. I went on my appointed rounds. Did my thing. Forgot about the fly like I forgot about the ants I probably accidentally walked on and killed, like I forgot the squirrel I'd seen hit on the highway last Monday, like I forgot about images of flattened snakes on country roads, like I'd forgotten other road-kill and crows swooping to pick at fresh meat after passing cars.

Preoccupied, I returned, entered the bathroom, slid open the window for a little air. Memory returned as I saw my fly. _My fly_? Why is it now my fly? I have no fly! The fly is its own fly! I have nothing to do with the fly! I observe, I do my thing, so get off my back already! God, get off my back. I can't help things in the world that trap flies between screens and windows so they can only fly in two dimensions and can't pursue their life-giving duties. Get off my back! Enough!

I slid the window open. The fly rested in a slightly different place and at a slightly different angle, as if it had been buzzing around a while. It had gone on a futile and exhausting attempt to fly in the third dimension – out! There was the fly on the screen looking out. Looking at freedom. Looking through the small, square, plastic bars of the screen of his personal, two-dimensional prison at trees, sky, flowers, wind, garbage, female flies and fly-world.

How sad, I thought, he's a fly, but can't fly away. I thought to open the screen to let him out to enter his three-dimensional fly-world once again, but I didn't. He wouldn't budge. He was stuck. Well, how much effort should I put in to save a doggoned fly, anyway? I'm big. I weigh 150 pounds and have a tiger of a brain compared to this little piece of flotsam. I'm important! I have things to do, bills to write, letters to send, calculations to make. Should I spend five minutes of effort trying to free the screen to free a fly? A fly whose eyes are trained only in one direction – toward the outside? His fly brain has no vision of what three-dimensional freedom might lie right behind him. His spirit is only directed outward to that for which he yearns.

Do I have time in my life for this fly? I know the fly is relatively high on the evolutionary scale for an insect. I have the chance of freeing him, but I'm too important to myself to do so. The window's slid away from the screen anyway, why doesn't he fly back into the room and stop looking outdoors. Why doesn't he seek freedom inside my little house? Perhaps he could eventually make it through an open door. Maybe he's in a state of dying, anyway.

Well, I don't have time for small things *(like flies)* as I never do, and sat down to write this ... I just looked up again. He's at the top of the screen – sideways, now, thinking it over. It's hard not being omnipotent.

JACK ON THE MOUNTAIN

*I*n keeping with writing just anything off the top of the head and in the beginning without anything to say, I sit and write. The one thing that must not be done – lift the pen off the page. I know if I blank the mind and relax, when I least expect it, I find myself in the middle of a thought. What the thought is always surprises me. Let it flow. That's what writing off the top of the head is all about.

Blanking the mind, then discovering the thought – blanking the mind, and then discovering the thought. It's kind of a meditation. Well – here goes ... *(blank)* ...

Boy! I hate fires. Those big brush fires that blacken thousands of acres and burn creatures, homes and people. We had one yesterday and it isn't over yet. I'm sure some of my friends were caught up in it. I know how that is. My family and I were caught up in one once. It was the pits and adversely affected our lives for years afterward.

Well, this morning I was sitting on top of Jack's mountain talking with Jack and he was drinking a little *"vino"* and watching the Little Sycamore fire 15 miles in the distance. Let me tell you about Jack's mountain. It's right off the paved, winding road at elevation about 3,000 feet and from there I can see the Pacific Ocean and all the nearby islands, the Bony Ridge mountain range, the Simi Valley mountains, Pitsch Canyon Village *(kind of a little Hobbit town), and* Calamigos Ranch. At twilight you can see the lights of Westlake Village and the abundant natural and mountainous beauty you would expect observable from a high mountaintop. It's the type of mountain that makes me feel I could walk across on top of projecting fog to island-like tips of surrounding mountains. *"You got a good view up here, Jack,"* I said, looking around with my hands in my jacket pockets.

We were sitting in the shade of Jack's trailer looking over the distant charred mountain range and the dusky red smoke billowing out to sea. Suddenly Jack was talking about rattlesnakes. *"I was bit by a rattlesnake once,"* Jack said*, "it was in Wyoming just after I was released from the Marine Corps. I was working for the U. S. Geodetic Survey Department mapping countryside."*

"They have big ones there?" I said, being companionable.

Jack continued, *"Yeah! Well, we were 500 feet down in a hot gully and I was carrying this 24 foot long stadia rod, you know, folded up, so's it was only 12 feet long? I had this stadia rod over my shoulder and I was following the Chief out of this hot ravine. Following, I don't know, about 20 feet behind him. Then this big rattler, <u>Whap</u>! – bites me on the shoe. Didn't rattle or nothin'. I was issued these 10 inch high Marine ankle boots. They give me those* *brand new boots and brand new Marine uniform two days before they discharge me into civilian life. I don't care. I just took 'em."*

"I guess there's a lot of waste in the military." I said.

"Yep! Anyway, this big rattler hits me – <u>*Whap*</u>*! – on the side of the shoe, you know, right where the seam is on the side?"* Jack raised his foot with its unbuckled loafer and showed me where the snake had struck.

"Did the fangs go through?" I asked.

"Huh?" Jack was preoccupied.

"Did the fangs go through your shoe?" I stayed with him.

"No. They didn't go through." Jack rocked back and forth trying to get comfortable.

"That's good." I want to hear the rest of this.

"I killed that rattler. Took my doubled up stadia rod and killed him by jamming his head with the end. When I got back to headquarters, the chief's boss said I should throw the shoes away. Brand new shoes! There might be poison on 'em, he said, and, "Throw that stadia rod away, too. We don't want t'get poison on anybody later on."

"Sounds wasteful." I uncrossed my legs, stretched them out, and put my hands behind my neck.

Jack said, *"That stadia rod musta cost 300 bucks and the shoes wasn't cheap either. But, what the Hell! So I got a new stadia rod and new boots. Hell, I didn't care."*

I crossed my legs again. *"That's too much."*

Jack continues, *"That's a crock of shit, though."*

"What?" Say I.

"That stuff about rattlesnake venom being poison. Hell! You could ingest that stuff and it wouldn't hurt you. It's protein, that's all it is. I could take the white of an egg, put it in a syringe and inject it in you and you'd be just as dead as if you got bit by a rattler. It's got to be <u>injected</u> in order to poison you. Hell, you could eat it and it wouldn't hurt you. Its just protein, that's all it is. Want some vino?"

"No thanks." Fine gray ash sifts out of the sky onto my pants and shoes. *"No thanks. I get sick on that stuff. "Probably what I drink would make you sick."*

"Why? What do you drink?" Jack was mildly curious.

"Water." Say I, amused.

"Yuck! Hell, the only thing I'd use that stuff for would be to put out that fire if it comes up here." Jack shifts uncomfortably in his chair, reaches for some vino, takes a sip, replaces it, looks out over the landscape. The smoke billows. The ashes drift. Things get quiet.

Pretty soon it's time to leave. I say, *"Thanks."*

Jack says, *"Sure. Come back any time."*

MARGIE AND THE TEN DOLLARS
(A story problem)

Margie Brigum, age 7, walks her dog 2-1/2 miles to cousin Peter's house, passing the country store every day at precisely 10:00 AM. It takes her 45 minutes to go all the way to Peter's house. One day, Mama Brigum gave Margie 10 dollars to buy groceries for cousin Peter's family. Margie did not arrive at cousin Peter's house for four hours that day, without groceries, although she did have chocolate peanut cluster crumbs at the corners of her mouth and felt sick to her stomach. She then lied, saying she lost the 10 dollars, while Cousin Peter noticed Margie went straight to the bathroom where the toilet could be heard flushing long into the night.

A) How many times will Mama Brigum give Margie ten dollars for groceries again?

B) Five dollars?

C) Any money at all?

MULBERRY TREES

*T*here was a young fellow who dug a hole in an empty, weed-covered field and covered it over with old boards to make a hut. While lying down inside, sunlight slits crossed his bare legs and he thought of six-year-old things.

Now visualize someone older, perhaps the same young fellow as an older person, as he lies on his couch in the study with his face to the ceiling, wrist to brow, making dreams, while through the mini-blinds, sunlight strips crossed his chest.

And he remembered the cherry tree flowering and the green cherries and the yellow cherries, ripe and juicy, and the eating, and the jarring of the jaw on hard pits.

Why is this interesting?
It's not, unless you're me.
What has this to do with the reader?
Nothing.
Then why not get on with something interesting?
Like what?
I'm sure you have tales to tell.
Well, yes. Let's see. Have you heard about the mulberry trees?

No. Is it interesting?

I think so.

Well, then, tell me about it.

Our family had two mulberry trees …

Yes. Go on.

They grew between the public sidewalk and the dirt street in front of our house.

Where did you live?

In a westerly suburb of Chicago in one of only two houses of Fairfield Avenue.

How many were in your family?

Four. My parents, my younger brother, and me.

Let's get on with it then. What about the
mulberry trees?

Well, we had two mulberry trees, oh, maybe fifteen feet high in the parkway next to the sidewalk, and in the spring the trees would bloom … I forget the kind of flower … but the trees would bloom and soon, hundreds of green, knobby berries would begin to form …

The little mulberries.

Yes. And as the summer progressed the berries would grow big, fat, and juicy.

And you ate them?

Yes. Mother would put them in a bowl and pour milk over them and the milk would turn purplish.

I bet they were good. And, then what?

Well, that's about it.

You said you had something interesting to tell me.

Well, that's it. That's the mulberry story ... Wait! The mulberries used to fall on the sidewalk and leave hundreds of purple stains on the concrete. And the birds ... the birds came by, by the dozens, and ate the mulberries right out of the tree.

This is the great mulberry story?

They'd scatter when I approached.

Is that all there is?

You didn't like it?

No. It was OK. I just thought ... well, we were talking about getting the reader involved in something sufficiently interesting to keep his mind on the reading.

That may be difficult.

NOTHING

I was telling Marge that once on a subject I had no problem writing about it. The problem was mainly the selection of what to write about, rather than whether or not I could write about it. I boasted I could write about <u>nothing</u> if necessary and asked her if I should show her. She said *"No! That's OK!"* I ignored her, but of course I would have to relate it to <u>something</u>. I might call it <u>Nothing</u>, by Roy Crandal. So, here's the tale of <u>Nothing</u>:

(I'll interview myself.)
What is nothing?
Nothing, of course.
            What does that mean?
It means <u>nothing</u> in relationship to <u>something</u>. Let's take a squirrel for instance. A squirrel has squirrel-like characteristics. Nothing is <u>not</u> a squirrel nor is it anything, therefore it is <u>nothing</u>. It doesn't run over the grass, its tail floating like a feather on the air, stop, grab something to eat, look around to see if there's danger, then scamper up a tree and disappear in the leaves. <u>Nothing</u> has <u>no</u> squirrel-like characteristics, nor in fact, does it have <u>any</u>

of the characteristics of <u>anything</u>.

Then nothing has no <u>meaning</u>?

Of course nothing has <u>meaning</u>.

How's that?

For instance, in talking about rocketing yourself to the moon after building a rocket ship from your do-it-yourself Home Depot kit, you torpedo yourself into outer space. The space you travel through is <u>nothing</u>. That means there isn't anything there, a scientific fact, beautifully expressed that has <u>meaning</u>.

Yes. I see. I think.

Nothing is also a <u>word</u> used to answer a question. For example, if I ask, *"What's on your mind?"* You may answer, *"<u>Nothing.</u>"* Whether your answer is true or not is difficult to say. There may be nothing on your mind, but you may <u>feel</u> hungry. In a sense, if you say <u>nothing</u> is on your mind, you've only told a half-truth. Though you may think nothing was on your mind, your organism may be telling you something else. For instance, you're <u>hungry</u>! Therefore, being hungry was part of your consciousness, which is part of your mind, therefore to answer <u>nothing</u> was on your mind is only a half-truth.

Consciousness is part of your mind?

Of course! Take itching, for example. If you're scratching a mosquito bite on the inside of your elbow with a hot wool sweater on, or if it's on your eyelid in that spot just above the lashes, you're conscious of an itch. Nerves from the itch, like a lightning bolt in a sudden storm followed

by a downpour, speed to your brain in panic, and you
become irrational and scratch.

I see. Anything else to say about nothing?
Nothing isn't here.

Where is it?
It isn't anyplace. It has no body, no brain, no sensitivity,
it can't see or hear or think or feel or go into spasms
of ecstasy from the aroma of a delicate Cabernet '65
that's a little saucy without being impertinent, and
you can't make an I-beam out of nothing to construct
a giant nonsense sculpture because it has no steel-like
properties. <u>Nothing</u> is a very descriptive word.

Isn't nothing <u>something</u> could be related to?
It usually is.

Then nothing is <u>something</u>.
I suppose so.

*Will you be getting the Pulitzer Surprise for
writing this?*
Probably.

A GOOD RUN

You see, at age 56 I can still jog for an hour or two without killing myself. Oh, I may be shot for the rest of the day *(or two)* but I suffer very little. I like to take the old *"bod"* for a little romp in the fields. I particularly like the valley behind our house, but I run the golf course, too, end-to-end, actually, then down the newly-graded road, then off to a plain, wide, beautiful valley. I hear the birds sing as I go, and the wind waves the grasses as I run the trail, and the breeze sweeping through the valley is clean and pure, for I go out early.

On Easter morning I took the route I'll be describing. The hills are crossed with bike trails. They usually follow the ridges, but sometimes they sweep straight down the wide slopes. These trails are ideal for running and on Easter morning I decided to run up a beautiful curving ridge. Presently, it got so steep I had to walk and instead of walking forward, I decided to exercise my *"reverse"* muscles and walk up backwards. Well, as I ascended, you should have seen the view. It got wider and longer and the winds were whipping up the hillsides and it blew my hair and on the bike trail I could see the shadow of myself with blowing hair.

The colors and shapes of the hills were magnificent shades of green, gray-green – green tinged with pink, or sometimes with slightly yellow tones. In the distance, the darker, stony-green mountains were bold and black and the sky was as blue as you'll ever want a sky to be. I took off my shirt so I could feel the wind against my chest as I backed up the hill. Occasionally I'd turn around and jog or walk forward. Once on the ridge, I had a 360 degree view of all there was. I could see valleys, ridges, and rooftops, tree groves, creeks, boulders, the freeway, and streets and canyons. Everything! It was a trip! And the ridge! The ridge was not a backbone ridge; it was more of a roller coaster ride. Up the ridge I went, over the top, down the steep road, straight up again, then down, then up and down again. A real ball! You see, I like to *"smell the flowers"* as I go. I don't jog so much as jog-walk. Well, the flowers were out, the birds and bees, the butterflies and beetles, and gophers and bunny rabbits. I guess everything was out on Easter Sunday. I didn't see any people, though. I was the only one. It was great! I took the old *"bod"* for a ride on my planet. I had good feelings then and it feels good to recapture them now. It's more fun to express what feels good. I feel lucky.

MORE JACK

Jack says a lot of weird things from time to time. I don't know why, but coming from him it seems dramatic. He owns the top of a mountain just off the highway, but hasn't the money or desire to build a house on it for himself. It seems strange to me for him to own such a magnificent lookout then just camp on it in a decrepit trailer and drink wine for the rest of his life. But Jack is what you'd call a bad alcoholic.

If I peek under his skin just a little I can see pain that makes me shiver. He has a foot long scar a half-inch from his navel that zigzags into his groin. It looks like a gore from the horn of a bull that he let heal *naturally*. The center of himself was ripped and twisted by something about which I am not sure I care to know, but I suspect that wound alone could depress the bravest of spirits. He has a steel plate in his left leg instead of a shinbone, too, but I suspect his emotional wounds are the worst.

Jack says he only sleeps four hours a night and he says, *"I'm a real light sleeper. If anyone taps the side of my trailer … (Jack makes a rapping motion with his knuckles) I wake up instantly. (Pause) And I always have my radio on, too. Yep! Twenty-four hours a day. I can't sleep unless the radio's on. If I lose power and it's night, I just can't sleep. It goes twenty-four hours a day."*

I try to imagine him at two o'clock in the morning and Jack's radio goes out and he awakes and a breeze is crying up the slopes through the wild sumac and toyon and the windblown stars are bright and there's no moon and Jack just lies there, awake, his bloodshot, irritated eyes open, staring, his mind just a little sober. Does his unbearable burden settle sickeningly into his wounded soul? Does he try not to think, but the feeling persists? Is that when he reaches for the vino? This is my own speculation and projection. Nevertheless …

Last night, a half-hour after sundown, Marge and I went up to Jack's lookout to check how far the fire might have spread. There it was, five miles away and seven miles long, flaming over the black hills with heavy white smoke streaming thousands of feet skyward. It looked like a Bosch painting of Damnation into which tiny borate bombers lumbered to drop their seemingly insignificant payload. Black, gnat-like helicopters observed, commented and controlled. The flames crawling along the ridges sometimes leapt a hundred feet into the air while others crept into valleys only to begin another upward sweep.

Jack was there with a scattered dozen or so concerned homeowners standing on the mountaintop near the trailer. The smell of smoke was irritating to the eyes and nostrils and fine ash drifted and settled on car hoods and shoulders. It was morbidly fascinating standing there, and Marge nestled in my arms seeking protection more that warmth. Thusly, while the world was burning, Jack, next to me in shirtsleeves and unwashed pants, said, *"Went over the hill a coupla weeks ago."*

Holding Marge and absorbed by the fire, I managed to say, *"What do you mean you went over the hill?"*

Jack shifted his feet. *"Went over and down around 300 feet."*

"You mean you fell down the hill, or what?" I gazed at the fire.

Slightly irritated, Jack said, *"No. Went off in my car. Fell 300 feet down the hill."*

"My God, Jack! That's terrible!"

Jack continues, *"I lay there for 18 hours. Couldn't move. Then the police showed up and a helicopter came and took me to the hospital."*

"Jesus Christ!" I said, *"You were 300 feet down the mountain for 18 hours. That's terrible. Were you unconscious?"*

"Part of the time." Jack folded his arms and glanced toward the fire.

"Were you bleeding? I was aware some of the watchers were leaving.

"Nope," Jack says*." I wasn't bleeding."*

"Were you trapped in the car?" I asked.

Jack rubbed his mustache. *"Nope, I got out, but then I passed out."*

"Why did you pass out? Did you hit your head?" I'm thinking this is a strange time to be telling me this.

"Nope. I got a steel brace in my leg that got twisted. I passed out from the pain. Then, I'd wake up and crawl some, then pass out. Finally, I crawled to the top of the hill and my buddy, John, helped me." (John is Jack's buddy who lives in what looks like a crashed camper left sitting down lower on the slope.)

"Well, I'm glad you're all right." The evening is darkening. There is another angry red flare-up that lights the billowing underbelly of smoke. A smoky odor penetrates my clothes and fine white ash quietly rains. Conversation lapses.

Jack says suddenly, *"I hit a boulder down there or I coulda gone another 400 feet."*

I'm curious about how he happened to drive over the cliff. *"Did you accidentally back over the hill and ride the car down backwards, or what?"*

"No, I went frontward. I stamped on the brakes, but hit some wet weeds and went over." Jack glanced quickly at me, then back at the fire.

I asked, *"Were you able to steer it on the way down?"* Marge shivers in my arms.

"Nope."

I'm awed by this story. *"Just rode her bouncing up and down 300 feet 'til you hit that boulder."*

"Yep."

"You know that boulder probably saved your life," I said.

"Yep."

"It's amazing you're still here. You've cheated death." I'm amazed.

"Yep." Said Jack.

(Then, I was going to exclaim, "You've been given another chance at life. God has spared you. Now you have time to do great things. You owe it to God and yourself, yes, and even me to do something productive, if not something worldly significant with your new life. The boulder and the miracle of your recovery is an omen of good things to come." But I stilled my tongue.)

I looked at Jack's irritated eyes, his unwashed clothes and tired shoulders. I felt how he must feel in his unbuckled black sandals, in his metal shin and scarred abdomen. The fire was raging out of control – a lot like all of us. Nothing anyone can do about an out-of-control brush fire, five miles out and seven miles long, especially at night. Pray, maybe.

Marge said rather loudly, *"Maybe we could evacuate some things from your office, just in case. Your copier your typewriter, your computer..."*

"Shhhhh," I said, suddenly feeling how financially well off I was compared to Jack.

Jack said, *"Hell, if that fire gets up here, I'll just grab a box of Marine discharge papers from the trailer and start away down that hill. "*

It was time to go.

MELVIN AND LUCY
(A story problem)

The ferry boat *SS Tulip* is in the middle of its 90 minute crossing of the Manataw River on its way to Bababa, Iowa, when four-year-old Lucy Brigum, who is practicing roller skating and eating a chocolate ice cream cone on the windy deck, is suddenly shoved by her six-year-old brother, Melvin. Her cone mashes up into her face as she sits – plunk – on the deck and begins to howl uncontrollably, whereupon Mama Brigum, rushing up, smacks Melvin up the side of the head three times causing him also to howl uncontrollably.

A) How many smacks up the side of the head does Melvin have to take before docking time?

B) How many new chocolate ice cream cones must be bought for Lucy?

C) How many new friends has Mama Brigum made during the crossing?

CRUISE STORY

*O*f course you know that Marge and I live in the hills above Malibu on a one-acre site with a small house and two work studios. I'm almost 74 and Marge just turned 68, and like it or not we are semi-retired and have reached that age when we can enjoy the promise of retirement. Why shouldn't we accept Marge's sister, Barbara, and her husband David's invitation to take a seven-day cruise aboard the Ryndam around the end of Baja? It was to be a maiden voyage by the Holland American Line in these waters, and we'd visit the little Mexican town of Loreto in the gulf, and on the way back, stop at La Paz and Cabo San Lucas. We would leave on Marge's 68th birthday, and this would be our gift to her that Marge has been saving nine months for.

Before we left, news of Hurricane Juliette was all over the TV. I exclaimed to Marge, *"Certainly a Major Cruise Line would not schedule a vacation trip sailing into a hurricane?"*

She assured me they would not! Hurricane Juliette would be well gone by the time we sailed. On the day we left, Juliette had just destroyed Cabo and was whirling into the Sea of Cortez. I felt better, but a question crossed my mind. *"How does anyone know when the hurricane season is really over? I'd not like to be caught between two hurricanes."*

To those who have been on cruises, you know what a cruise ship is like, but on departure day I was unprepared for what I saw. On the gangway while boarding the ship, I caught brief views of black and white sides towering 11 stories. At 777 feet long, I was astounded that in length it was equivalent to over two-and-a-half football fields. I couldn't wait to run all over the ship, end to end, top to bottom.

We had been forewarned there would be an *"abandon ship"* drill immediately upon boarding. After settling in our cabins it was mandatory that we break into groups, don life jackets, and go on deck for the emergency rehearsal. The practice took 45 minutes, and I remember standing in a crowd among different sized people in yellow life jackets; women and children in front, men behind. I couldn't see out! We were to tie the thing-bunky around our waste and if the pneumatic pump failed, blow on the whataya-call-it. While listening to our leader I was thinking, *"Surely he must be kidding!"*

Marge and I and Barbara and David took easily to pampering by the polite Indonesian crew. The ship was gigantic and I had only the slightest sensation of floating on water as we moved steadily and majestically out to sea. After a wonderful dinner at our specially-reserved table in the huge dining room, I became melodramatic. *"Long since are faded the slim and flickering lights of civilization and we are lost in the silence and blackness of open ocean."* Actually, we were just off Tijuana.

Our accommodations were excellent and we slept excitedly through the night. Early in the morning, sunlight streamed through our four-foot-square porthole, and we saw the hazy mist of morning rising from the ocean, with its reliable foamy wake steadily and noiselessly flowing at 20 knots.

There were two swimming pools; one interior, open to the sky, and one exterior, with pool, deck and lounge chairs freely sweeping across the aft. There were two dance pavilions on floors seven and eleven. There was a smoking lounge and wet bar, gymnasium, shopping mall, gambling casino, Las Vegas-type theater with surrounding balcony for live shows, motion picture theater, two luncheon cafeterias either side of the ship with long windows facing the sea and a full two-story formal dining room below the aft pool. There were walking decks, and on the bow, four observation platforms on separate floors and a jogging deck open to the sky surrounding an immense skylight that opened and closed over the interior pool. Everything was built meticulously and luxuriously. It was a floating hotel; a paradise on water.

We spent another day and night enjoying the facilities, and on the evening of our third night, guests were requested to come to dinner in formal dress. At the elevator lobby we stepped out onto a plush carpet leading to a beautifully appointed dining hall with surrounding balcony. The two floors were connected by a luxurious and dramatic stairway winding up through an interior atrium. At twilight, both dining floors overlooked the gray and fading light of the sea. Over 500 people arrived and circulated through to assigned tables. Another 500 were to arrive at seven. We had a lovely meal, and the gentle chattering noises of 500 people mixed softly with the tinkling of silverware and glasses. There was plenty of wine and many were in a state of spirituous relaxation.

It was time for dessert! The busboy had distributed hot decaf with cream, and all the tuxedoed and gowned guests were primed for truffles, exotic fruits, and layered ice cream cakes decorated with stringy, wine-colored toppings. Our spoons were lifted in anticipation of the first ambrosial bite when the Captain's resonant voice suddenly came over the speakers. He sounded serious and worried, which to me meant ominous. A few forks dropped to their plates while jovial clatter quieted and an attentive silence crept over the audience. In a low, strong voice, the Captain said:

"What I'm about to say may be taken uncomfortably by some of you, but I beg your indulgence. Another hurricane is moving swiftly toward us at 100 miles to the southwest. We are in no danger at present, but to avoid the possibility of being trapped in the gulf, I'm not going to continue to Loreto as planned, but will dock at Pichelingua. (The La

Paz port) By that time more information will be available and we may move on to Loreto or, if that's not possible, stay in La Paz until the storm passes. We will definitely <u>not</u> be stopping at Cabo San Lucas, since I have just learned Hurricane Juliette has destroyed the roads and docking facilities. I'm sorry to burden you with this information, but thank you for your attention. I'll keep you informed."

There was a silence in the dining room before a quieter and more serious conversation resumed. Marge asked me how the Captain's announcement made me feel. I said, *"I'm scared to death and about to throw up."* I thought to myself, *am I not the protector of my little group of four; leader of the women past their physical prime, assistant to David who is in a wheelchair? I am supposed to show bravery! I am <u>not</u> supposed to be scared to death! I am supposed to say, 'I feel fine! Boy, this dessert's good! What's up for tomorrow? Wow! Nice ship!'*

Lots of things raced through my mind. *(What's all this 'trapped inside the gulf' business? I presume by high waves. How does the ship do in high waves? If we're in high waves, does that mean we're going to go down? I don't <u>want</u> to go down! Why did he tell us now? Was it so urgent the Captain had to tell us before dessert? The dining room windows look unusually black! I think I feel the ship moving on a swell right now; first indication of the new storm. How large the Titanic looked in dock and how miniscule at sea. The dripping stern lifted hundreds of feet out of water, then the ship went straight down like an iron* *bar, breaking in half on the way! How would a cruise ship handle a hurricane?*

I'd examined sections of the ship and discovered, though it rose eleven stories above the waterline, it extended perhaps only three stories below the waterline. In my mind, I questioned thusly:

Who would design a top-heavy boat? Being top-heavy, perhaps in a storm it would roll on its side and float, one side up and one side down. Then only half the lifeboats would be available. How would we launch them? How far is shore? I think the captain said 14 miles. I can't swim that far! Is the water cold? How could I swim 14 miles and save Marge, let alone Barbara and David? Maybe we could float for hours clinging to a piece of debris. In storm waves the Captain would probably face the ship into the wind. We'd be bobbing fore-and-aft, bow submerging, while rolling violently side-to-side. Would everybody throw up? I'd throw up! Are sharks attracted to vomit? I thought this would happen! I'm glad we practiced "abandon ship!" What about a crowded lifeboat in a hurricane? We're caught between two hurricanes! Cruise lines did schedule us through the hurricane season! I remember a movie. A big ship was caught in a storm, rolled over, but continued to float upside down. Inside, people crawled up to the bottom and breathed the stuffy, trapped air. Rescuers couldn't drill a hole through the bottom, because the air would spout out like whale spume and the ship would quietly disappear into Davy Jones' locker. Then there was the Joseph Conrad story. This stubborn captain decided to drive his ship right through a violent hurricane. The barometer was impossibly low! They blasted through one side, all about dead, then came into the eye, looked up to see the stars, then slammed into the other side, the wind blowing counter! Months later, the ship was found empty and destroyed like a drifting ghost. Have they made any improvements since the 18th century? Is our captain stubborn? Are there sharks?

We went to Pichelingua; saw La Paz, then to Loreto where we had a delightful time and took lots of pictures, then sailed back around Baja to San Diego. We didn't feel or see any hurricane. The ride was smooth. I'm glad I went on the cruise. It had its moments.

NORBERT AND THE ELEVATOR
(A story problem)

If 170 pound Norbert Brigum stepped off the 100th floor of the Metropolitan Life Insurance building into the *"down"* elevator with six others averaging the same weight, and at the same time the supporting cable snapped and the elevator plunged basement-ward, leaving Norbert's *"nerd"* hat hovering 18 inches above his head, calculate the exact moment Norbert must leap horizontally through the not-yet-open door, missing the concrete *"in-between"* floors to tumble safely into the pants and stockings of the awestruck persons waiting for the *"down"* elevator on the 37th floor, if the car plummeted past each opening at an acceleration rate of 50 feet-per-second-per-second.

Alternate question: If the remaining six passengers all leap 20 inches off the floor one second before basement impact, how much would all six weigh while in the air?

WIMPY CHIPS

Did this ever happen to you? You're at a party with your girlfriend. You don't know many people there. Maybe one or two are friends of your friends who aren't there, and your date doesn't know them either. And there is always the dip; guacamole or sour cream or cheese or whatever, sitting on the coffee table in front of a crowd on the sofa. Next to it is a bowl of potato chips.

The idea is to scoop the dip with the potato chip. I guess this is a good way to eat dip. Everybody scoops it with great success, especially females. And since it's always crowded around the dip, it takes me a while to get up my nerve, but feeling silly and a little awkward at having no dip to munch on, I plan a way around all those arms and legs to get that dip. Of course, to me, it's important to look cool, even slight macho, in order to *"get"* the women and affect a silent *"watch out"* to other males.

Balancing my drink carefully, I step over a leg, duck a gesture, and get the chip. Now for the dip. I'm there! I dip my chip! The chip breaks! I'm mortified. My forehead begins to sweat. That potato chip has broken off and is lying, half buried, in the dip. Obscenities to Laura Scudder's or Frito Lay or chip companies in general! How can they do this to me? Here I am, a good-lookin' stud, macho man, dipping his chip and it breaks! What am I supposed to do? Look around at the ladies, grin, and say, *"Ha! Ha! Broke my chip?"*

No! I try to square my shoulders, but can't because I'm stooping and trying to go for the dip again. This time I go knuckle deep into the guacamole, submarining for the chip that has become inextricably mired in *(obscenity)* dip. Repeated attempts only work my chip deeper into the muck. My fingers are a mess. I'm spilling my drink. I'm off-balance and I'm not the least bit hungry. I had a sandwich before I came over. I could go foodless for three days without a pang. One more bite of anything and I'll throw up. Why did I go for the dip?

I think to myself, I'll fake it. I'll pretend I got the dip on the chip, eat my fingers while retreating and resign myself to having been doodled by the chip companies. Well, we all survive these little embarrassments. They are part of life. *"If you can't stand the pain, get out of the game. Right?"*

If I were a chip company, I'd come out with a 26 gauge galvanized iron chip; one guaranteed not to break off in the dip. Of course, there were <u>corn</u> chips at the party, but out of reach. It could be argued I should have gone for the corn chips. Maybe so.

Afterward, I got as far away from the dip as possible. When my hostess looked me in the face and asked, *"How about some more dip?"*

I said, *"No thanks."*

She said, *"You simply have to try Jo Jo's dip. It's simply fabulous!"*

I said, *"No thanks, I've already tried it."* (*I remembered it tasted like dog poo-poo.*)

She grabs me by the hand, hauling me toward the wimpy chips and *dog* dip. I go with her, stumble through the people guarding the dip, scoop up a handful of guacamole, defiantly stare at everybody, pretend to wash my armpits, and beat it out the alley. My date left with somebody else. Next time, it's beer only and to heck with the dip and wimpy chips.

FAITH

Viewed through the most sophisticated microscope, matter, that final concrete, indivisible substance upon which I'd welcome basing my philosophy, is absent. Each of the atoms is made of protons and neutrons with electrons swirling around them. Is then a rock alive? And when you take the most elaborate microscope and examine the atom, or protons or neutrons or electrons that won't stand still for experiments, as the ultimate building block for all things, and they disappear into arbitrary infinities of nothingness, life seems like a thought or kind of music.

Perhaps the big bang theory is plausible since, where there's no substance, what isn't there occupies no space and everything could be jammed together with plenty of room. And recent investigations have shown *"no-see-ums"* in space called *"dark matter"* that form in clouds holding clusters of galaxies together, while invisible and undetectable dark energy pushes galaxy clusters apart at accelerating speed. It is true that matter attracts matter, but stars, planets and moons of galaxies account for only a fraction of the gravity necessary to hold them together. Dark matter, of course, accounts for keeping them where we can see them. My philosophy is that we might be in a musical dream made up of our waterish earth, the moon, sun, and our brilliant night sky, and though we continually discover more, we continually know less.

Assuming we are in a miraculous dream with galaxies, suns, planets, land and water, plants, animals and humans, and assuming we live in this miraculous terrarium, protected from the frigid, life destroying minus 270 degrees centigrade by a thin, deteriorating layer of gas, what then, I must ask myself, would be my philosophy?

Answer: I accept that trees grow to fulfillment, mate, re-seed and die, as do all plants, humans and animals. I accept that a table, though possibly a musical dream, is in fact a hard substance to me, because that's the way it looks and feels. My philosophy must start with my life. Parts of life have faith and trust that are the prerequisites for love. When life is good, love is the key ingredient. Without faith and trust there is no love and life would not be good. To a greater or lesser degree, lack of love is evil. Good, then, defines evil. Without evil there can be no good and without good there can be no evil. Love and evil are interdependent. Therefore, to a greater or lesser degree, I have faith there will be love and no love, hate and no hate and trust and know there will be good and evil.

ELOISE AND THE RIGGED SCALE
(A story problem)

Mama Brigum's friend, Eloise, who is five feet tall, is a teensy bit overweight now and then and has rigged a special scale with a police siren, a recorded voice that screams, *"Oingo Boingo! Oingo! Boingo!"* and a 16 ounce boxing glove set to automatically punch her in the face for every three pounds she weighs over 180.

Eloise has transgressed over the weekend and, headgear in place, is about to step on the special scale. I suspect she is 12 pounds over the maximum. If I'm right, how many punches to the face can she expect to absorb from the 16 ounce glove?

Alternate question: How many pounds overweight would she have to be for a knockout if it always takes 48 blows?

HE WHO PLANTS A TREE

I wish to examine a line by a poet who asks, *"What does he do, who plants a tree?"* He plants a tree, of course, but this is so obvious, the poet must have had something else in mind. *"What does he do, who plants a tree?"*

He may be planting gopher food. I've spent dollars, and I mean big bucks on special fruit trees, planted them, watered them, covered them, protected and prayed for them, only to see them yanked out of sight in broad daylight by a gopher, and he only ate the STEM!

One day there's a young tree, it's springtime, it's budding and looking fresh and perky, getting ready for a big summer, and the next day the trunk is half way down the hole and the leaves are dying. I'm so mad I could *KILL!*

But back to, *"What does he plant, who plants a tree?"* Let's assume the gophers don't get the tree and it grows to be big and spreading, like the classic chestnut tree with the fat trunk. People come along and carve their initials or *"Joe's an obscenity,"* or something worse. So what he plants could be a place for vulgar comments. I'm sure the poet didn't have this in mind. No! He probably visualized the lofty branches reaching skyward, the twittering leaves in the balmy breezes, the thrust of the trunk toward archetypal greatness. He also planted future wood for tract houses; export lumber, a source for newspaper, a market for rakes and bug spray.

But negativity is not productive. We know what he planted don't we? He planted his own hope. He acknowledged a force created by a higher power, His act an affirmation of life. He saw this sturdy trunk as a bulwark against the raging storms, or its stark silhouette resolute in the deadly droughts. He saw the fruit as a gift to hungry strangers marching wearily through the tedium of existence – such as when looking for a job. He imagined his tree giving shade to the tired passerby, or a shelter to Sunday picnickers, or a climbing place for children. *"I think that I shall never see a poem lovely as a tree. A tree whose..."* I forget the rest.

I think he who plants a tree, plants his best wishes for himself. And when the planter's life is done he can be buried under the spreading, leafy branches of the tree he planted and this will be his lovely everlasting resting place and he will make good fertilizer.

OUT ON A LIMB

*I*t's nice out on a limb. I feel free. The wind flutters the leaves and cools my face. My grip is strong and I can see the meadow, the stream, the mountains, the clouds, and in the distance, the lights of the city where lives take place. *(Not mine.)* The city lights twinkle at dusk as I sit on my limb eating a fried egg sandwich on rye. Where did I get the sandwich, you say? Why, from my under-counter refrigerator roped and tied to the trunk.

The tree is tall, you see, and I live on a high limb. I have a large hammock slung up there, and sometimes I snuggle with Marge and urge her to stay the night with me. *(Out on the limb.)* She loves me and sometimes she stays.

The night is refreshingly cool and the stars are unusually bright. Sometimes they spiral and swirl like a Van Gogh painting. During those times we snuggle deep under the covers and tell each other stories, unmindful there is nothing beneath us but hard, rocky soil and a slow mountain stream.

When she stays, in the early morning the first shafts of morning sun awaken us. We arise and after tea and hot cereal get into our work clothes to leave for the city. It is then we discover we're out on a limb. Marge would prefer sleeping nearer the trunk, but these days I feel restless. I have this urge to explore the farther reaches of the limb. That is, climb farther out. I can see around a few branches and if I take care and with a little luck, I think I can make it farther out. At times I look down and become frightened, though I have learned that when climbing, it's best to keep your eye on what's solid around you. I have examined the branch attachment to the trunk and it appears solid from what I can see. Of course I haven't x-ray eyes and cannot tell about the interior condition of the branch. And so, though I move farther out, there is some anxiety I naturally carry with me. It is my hope I will discover something even more beautiful than what I am experiencing now, perhaps a better way of seeing things. I do know I feel vulnerable on the ground and it's nice out on a limb.

CRAIG ELLWOOD

I don't know why the subject of clothes cracks me up so much. I suspect it is because I am painfully unaware of my feelings that I'm a poor Chicago boy. But why analyze it? I accept who I am, right? Wrong! I met Craig Ellwood one time. Craig, the great white architectural designer, the house and small commercial architect who has made *"significant"* contributions to architecture in Southern California. *(And, therefore, in the <u>world</u>!)* Craig, with the salt-and-pepper hair, the strong, aesthetic face, the tall tennis figure with the polished ankle boots, the leather jacket, the expensive sports car. He's not only handsome and intelligent, but sensitive, athletic, and above all, creative. *(This may not be who he really is, but it is how I make him out to be.)* Craig Ellwood has been published in all the important architectural magazines, touting his new innovations in steel construction for homes and the women who loved him. He is dashing, daring, devil-may-care and a risk taker who always wins.

Well, I met him one day on one of his jobs. A contractor, Roy Norvelle, who had worked for both of us, introduced me to him. My heart was pounding. I was going to actually meet the great personage on one of his own brilliant jobs. I was actually going to see him strolling meaningfully among the steel members and laminated timbers of his own great creation. In fact, I couldn't get out of it. He showed up unexpectedly, stepped out of his XKE, and walked on the job.

"Doug, this is Craig. Craig, this is Doug." When I shook hands his grip was strong and manly with a warmth and forthrightness that showed me I was *not* cut from his mold. My hand was sweaty and I didn't get a good grip. He shook three of my fingers. I ventured a toothy grin. *(I have this one front tooth that sticks way out.)* His teeth, when he smiled, were even and white. I was aware of shoes I'd worn on my jobs for a year that were run over at the heels and my sock was a quarter turn over my instep and a ball of material was wadded up under my metatarsal arch.

"Glada meecha Craig," I mumbled. Norvelle and I followed him through his job; his lean body stepping cleanly over each plank and pipe. I wore my shirt out to hide where my stomach fat rolling over my belt forces the waste-band white of my pants to be exposed to the outside. Well, we got through it. Roy, my contractor friend, mentioned to Craig that I was an architect, too.

Craig said, *"Oh, yeah?"* That was the end of our conversation. He left.

But, you know, I don't feel so bad. I've done some pretty good work, too. And though I may not be as well known as Craig, I've had my moments. It's just that, well, he looks the part so terrifically, and he takes risks and I admire him for that. I didn't feel he was interested in me, though. And so, in the last analysis, I have him, but he doesn't have me. I ask you, who's the richer?

VAST MISTAKE

"I see blowing up the world as a vast mistake." Roy Crandall made the preceding quote to his friends over coffee on November 9, 1981. Perhaps it wasn't his greatest insight, but it was the best for the day.

Upon hearing this statement, one of the friends sniggled, one hand covering his mouth. Others were to laugh out loud at the obviousness of this thought. One intelligent person asked, *"For whom?"* Meaning for whom it would be a mistake?

Mr. Crandall replied, *"Why, for everybody."*

When asked to elucidate, he said *"Everybody would be dead because there would be no land to stand on, nor forests or trees or oceans or streams of fish or birds. There might be clouds, however, but not the same kind as we see in the heavens today."*

Someone asked, *"How did you come to know all this?"*

Crandall replied, *"It came to me in a flash while waiting for the stoplight to change."*

One of the guests, sipping her coffee, then asked, *"What can we do about it?"*

Roy said, *"I guess we'll all just have to see the other*

person's point of view, value it a as a rarity, and protect it as if it were a priceless jewel."

"Why do that?" Cried those who were listening.

Roy replied, *"Because mankind has already tried NOT listening to others' points of view and the world is about to make a vast mistake. Sometimes our own point of view can blur or even obliterate the others' point of view."*

Groaning and sighing arose from those who heard Roy's answer as they shifted their weight, first to this foot, then to that. *"Yeah, but ... yeah, but ... yeah, but ..."* Said one intelligent person and followed each *"yeah, but ..."* with a reasonable question like, *"What if I see others' points of view and value them as a rarity, but they don't see my points of view and value them as a rarity?"*

Roy proceeded with the following story:

A man called up his brother on the phone, but his brother didn't answer, so he tried and tried until, for whatever reason, the brother <u>did</u> answer the phone and then they communicated.

"What did they say to each other?" Said a little boy standing nearby.

"I don't know," said Roy. *"But the moral is, 'If you can't communicate right this moment, you must keep trying.'"*

"Woof! Woof! That makes sense!" Barked a dog, taking off his hat and scratching his head with one paw. People threw napkins at the dog until, yelping, he ran out of the house.

"I see blowing up the world as a vast mistake." This

statement by Roy Crandall on November 9, 1981 was written on a piece of paper by Roy's wife, along with his opinion that, in order to keep our beautiful world, others' points of view are going to have to be seen as a rarity and protected as we would protect a priceless jewel.

(With regard to Carl Rogers, who, in his paper Do We Need "A" Reality? This thought is so clearly developed. From A Way of Being, Houghton Mifflin Company, Boston, MA, 1980, pages 96 to 108)

HEROES OF THE EIGHTIES

*H*eroes are an important concept to me because they have qualities and attributes I admire and wish I possessed. I don't remember the name of my first hero, but I remember his slouching stance. He was a 15 year-old baseball player standing over the plate ready to belt one out of the park. I was nine and he was one of the big guys. He was too skinny, never said anything, and had a terrible slouch. When at bat, he'd usually make a two-base hit between first and second or second and third. Occasionally he'd connect with a fastball and crack a homer that flew straight over the outfielder's head. As an underhand pitcher, he'd wind up and throw the ball so fast you couldn't see it, and when in the outfield he appeared relaxed and stationary, but when action was called for, in effortless grace, he delivered miracles. He slouched. He was silent. Hands on hips, glove outstanding, he'd spit now and then and always came up with big plays. I lacked his superior abilities in high school, but borrowed his slouch.

When I was 14, my second hero was a manly-looking high school swimmer and pole vaulter named Swede Drangsholt. He showed me by example how to pole vault.

I didn't know him well and he wasn't an especially good student, but intelligence didn't matter to me in those days. I just admired him and wanted to be like him. Of course, where Swede was tall and lanky with broad shoulders, I was short and stocky. I never saw him after he graduated.

In high school, Don *"Mac"* McGregor put me in touch with an author named Jack London. He'd written a book with a character named Martin Eden who rose from squalor to success by endless studying and determination. Eventually he became the perfect man, except when he came to know everything, he decided there was nothing more to live for and drowned himself by swimming straight down a hundred feet or so in the middle of the ocean. I'd not go *that* far, not only since I'd never learn everything in the world anyway, but also I liked the idea that incorporated the idea of infinite self-improvement. My old high school buddy, *"Mac"* McGregor, is also one of my heroes for being himself and a reader that gave me the book.

In college, I studied architecture and you'd think I'd have developed a few architectural heroes, but except for Wright, Mies and a slight affinity toward a French architect, Le Corbusier, who claimed it was *his* office because *he* swabbed the toilets, I had none. Then I moved to California, got married, had three kids and started a business. I can't think of any real heroes that affected me during that time. 30 years went by. And now I'm old and seem to have more heroes now than ever.

William Blake is a recent hero because he was an artist-philosopher and stood by his religious *(or anti-religious)* convictions. They were contrary to the society's religious ideas at the time, but I liked the originality of his artwork and his vivid written imagination. *(Tiger, tiger, burning bright in the forests of the night, ... And when the stars sent down their spears and watered heaven with their tears did he smile his work to see? Did he who made the lamb make thee?)* I wanted to be like Blake.

T. S. Eliot's poem, *The Love Song of J. Alfred Prufrock*, affected me deeply. *("In the room the women come and go, talking of Michelangelo ... We grow old. We grow old. We shall wear the bottoms of our trousers rolled ... We have lingered in the chambers of the deep, by sea girls wreathed with seaweed red and brown 'til human voices wake us and we drown.")* And then I admired the late 20th century poets, Theodore Roethke and Pablo Neruda, and the writer, Zane Grey, too, though he may not be as fashionable a hero to others. Nevertheless, he is to me for his brilliant descriptions of the desert and his love for the colorful beauties of the old west.

Then there's the comic-dramatic genius, Woody Allen, one of my heroes for his masterful linking of philosophy, psychology and humor. And again, the comic quartet of Carol Burnett, Harvey Korman, Tim Conway and Vickie Lawrence deserves a place on my list, and the ribald Englishman, Benny Hill, slides in for another home run. *(It may be most of my heroes are comedians. What does that tell you?)* Certainly Garrison Keillor, America's tallest comedian, claims a place as do the short stories of Donald Barthelme. These are certainly two of my present heroes.

In architecture, I must list two architects, Gordon Drake, and my mentor, Kenneth Nishimoto, who taught me about proportion and repose in architecture. Musically, I have to choose Bela Bartok, whose musical being seems to come from another plane. Artistically, I must include Paul Klee for his investigation of small worlds, small feelings, small ideas, and nuances of idea, color, line, and composition. The bulk of his small things make him historically BIG!

Unsurprisingly, my dad comes into the list of heroes. He never said a word, yet by example is one of my greatest heroes. He showed me how to work a little harder for my boss and heaped upon me great quantities of unconditional love. For a psychological hero, I would choose John Powell, who wrote, among other books, Unconditional Love. His way of putting eternal truths in a simple way shows his unassailable genius. Yes, and David Viscott would count as a powerful one, because he devoted his life to caring, counseling, and teaching others.

To reach hero status for me, it is not enough that I have been merely affected by someone; I have to want to incorporate them, or portions of them, into my own being. I have to feel my hero and I are soul mates. His *(or her)* deeds, abilities, points of view, and personality must be absorbed into my spirit and assimilated easily. I shall gather heroes like flowers.

BUDDHA AT THE BALL GAME

Come on, gang, let's go!

I do not understand this. Is there a gang on the playground? Where are they going? From where have they come?

Boy! I hope the Red Sox win!

I do not see a boy. Oh! There is a boy with red hair! They must call him Red Socks. But, who is Win? Why should Red Socks Win, whoever he is? I do not understand.

Yahoo! A home run!

Someone must run home? Does that mean his mother is calling him? And what is this word, "Yahoo?" Do you suppose it means, "yes, whom?" Perhaps whom is the red-haired boy with the sticks who must go home because his mother is calling him?

Go get 'em, team!

Go get 'em, team? I do not understand. Team is a breakfast cereal, I believe. Am I to suppose he means to get some Team? Perhaps the gang on the field did not have breakfast. Will they have milk, too? I did not hear them say go get 'em, milk. Perhaps juice will do.

Slide, darn it, slide!

I do not understand. How could a slide be darned? Do

they mean a children's slide? I would not send my child down a slide that was darned. Why did he not say, darn the slide? I do not see a slide. Perhaps he means down the river. I see no river either. This is very disconcerting.

Boo! Kill the umpire!

Kill the umpire? Who or what is an umpire? What did he do that they should kill him for it? Perhaps they mean Empire. Kill the British Empire? That would not be sportsmanlike. Neither the umpire nor the Empire should be killed without a fair trial. I see no judge or jury out there. I am baffled.

Wow! Top 'O the ninth!

Wow! A doggy says, "Bow! Wow!" Does he refer to a doggy then? And top of the ninth. Why nine? Why not seven or 23? Nines have no top or bottom. If you turn a nine over, you get a six. If you turn a six over you get a nine. But where does sex fit into all this?

Three and two on the batter!

Three and two on the batter? Why not just say five? What is batter? Could he mean five on the cake batter? Perhaps he means five _in_ the cake batter. But what? Chocolate chips? Walnuts? And why only five? I would put many chips and many nuts in my batter. But, each to his taste.

One more strike and he's out!

Will they strike him senseless, then? Strike him until he's unconscious? Strike him until his lights go out? What a merciless happening. I would that I should not see this foul deed. And yet, they seem so happy.

Think of it. Two hitters in a row!

Two people who do hit in a row? This is very strange, indeed. Six or seven should make an excellent row. Two is not much of a row of anything. Perhaps they mean row your boat. Or, row, row, row your boat gently down the stream … But, what means, "No hitters?" Could they mean not to hit the two who row the boat? Very strange. Very curious.

What a game!

What a game? I too, do not understand what is a "game." Robin Hood killed game in Sherwood Forest. Perhaps, they are asking what kind of game they should acquire for the feast tonight. I am hungry, also. And very tired. And very confused. I think I shall retire from this challenging event and rest myself. Goodbye.

MORE FLIES

*T*oday I think I have nothing to say. I eat my sandwich. I drink my buttermilk. I look out the window. The Spanish Broom is a riot on the hillside and while I write, I smell their fragrance. I'm lucky to have my space. Some people don't have their space. I was telling my grown daughter, Viv, this morning, all she needs is a studio in which to work and a 1,000 square-foot warehouse to store her stuff. Sometimes I think that's all anybody needs.

Not to change the subject, but it's been nice this winter without flies. Now, here it is, May eighth, and behold, I'm observing the first fly of the season. I hate to kill flies and ants. The first thing I think of when I see a fly is *"Swat that fly!"* But the way they look all squished against the wall. *"Yuck!"* But then, they really don't hurt anybody. People say they carry diseases, I guess, because they're not afraid to walk around on things we'd never walk around on. In some cases, you'd think the smell would make them dizzy and they'd pass out. But I guess flies are short on nose, and long on eyes.

They have about a million as I hear told and that's probably the biggest rumor of the century. But I've seen pictures in National Geographic and they're supposed to show the <u>truth</u>. *(No lying in National Geographic. That magazine is the most truthful of all periodicals.)* But back to flies. Flies have big pad-like feet. Like, if it were on a human it would be size 18 to 24. Really big! And when they walk around on gooey, smelly stuff, like around the big steel trash containers behind markets; let's say they're walking around on rotten fruit, let's say squashed, rotten avocados, they don't sink in that far, but sure pick up a lot of goo on their feet.

I wonder. Do they eat that stuff off their feet? Come to think of it, do flies have a mouth? Do they have teeth? Do they have cavities? Do they have bridgework? Or even fly dentists? Maybe they just suck it up through a disgusting, nose-like sucker-snout. Sort of sniff it into their bodies.

I've never heard a fly scream, either. Usually you just whack 'em one. <u>Smack</u>! And it's all over, Louie! They die brave. But then, if they haven't any vocal cords, then what do you expect? I bet they were scared to death when they saw that swatter come down just an instant before they met their maker.

I can imagine, I'm swatting this fly, see, and just before I hit it, the fly knows he's a goner and I hear this little, shrill shriek. *"Aaoooaeee!"* Then, <u>Whap</u>! And it's all over, and that little scream *"Aaoooaeee!"* resounds in my mind after he's dead, over and over, *"Aaaeee! Aaaeee!"* And that horrible <u>Whap</u>! And the fly has departed the world quite unexpectedly. I feel awful about that. Like what if I was a fly and a big giant human ten million times bigger that me hit me with a fly swatter. Believe me! I'd go, *"Aaaaooooee!"* too, and meet my maker.

Question: Do flies have a God? What does a fly's God look like? Probably like a great big oversized fly. The Big Fly in the Sky with Billions of Eyes. And fly heaven? There's a place I don't want to go.

PENTACHAETA LYONII

I care about the Pentachaeta Lyonii. Long may she reign? A tiny endangered plant species, that according to the Coastal Commission, might live in the bottom of my watercourse. It's not in any of the standard books. A taxonomist might know a Pentachaeta Lyonii if she saw one. Perhaps she'll find one down by my creek. I use the word creek loosely, for it's dry this time of year, especially with minimal winter rains.

The boulders are huge and hoary at the bottom of my creek. Water spills and tumbles around them during heavy rains. At those times they are red-brown and filled with tide pool pockmarks. The birds must love the tide pools on the boulders in the creek bed when it rains. One sycamore tree winds its way skyward through live oak branches. The textures and shapes of the two leaf types are different; the sycamore leaf, larger, fuzzy and lighter green; the live oak leaf, smaller and shiny with prickles. Dead leaves of all kinds fill the creek bottom, toyon, sumac, bush mallow, ceanothus, chamise, coyote bush, etc.

Over there is a fine stand of poison oak. Talk about health? Just look at the poison oak plant. It must be at

least sixty million years old. Probably born shortly after
the huge meteorite struck the Yucatan Peninsula 65 million
years ago, causing worldwide darkness and a frigid planet
resulting in the extinction of the dinosaurs. What could
possibly affect poison oak?

And the creek bottom creatures? There must be
spiders, ants, beetles, flies, wasps, caterpillars, butterflies,
dragonflies, and moths in the bottom of the creek. There
must be rats, mice, moles, gophers, and other burrowing
things. There must be rabbits, squirrels, coyotes,
opossums, an occasional bobcat, and raccoons as well as
rattlers, gopher snakes, king snakes, and garden snakes. In
the live oaks and sycamores there must be owls, hawks,
crows, finches, red-winged blackbirds, and in the nearby
grassy plane, the meadowlark. And these creatures must
have daily events; tasks done on a daily basis to maintain
their lives. All of them interacting with the foliage, the
creek, and themselves forming an ecology. And for these
creatures, mornings must be different than afternoons,
twilight or night. Some are early risers, some late, and as
the day's heat cools and the first zephyrs of a night breeze
flutter the leaves on the trees, things in the creek bottom
change.

The owl, sleeping all day, awakens in the nighttime,
seeing wonderfully in the darkness. He's a terrible foe to
smaller creatures of less advantage, like mice and gophers
and small snakes. At predawn, coyotes prowl the hills or sit,
alert, ready to pounce. Watch out, hares, you are chief food

for coyotes. And in the early morning, the snakes awaken *(I guess)* and slither through weed bottoms in search of some shocked victim, or sit deathly still to mortally attack some unhappy prey. The ants, oblivious to all creatures, including almost to life itself, work and store and kill and drag and travel. The ant, the Promethean, absorbed in daily tasks, seems unaware of other living things. Or, perhaps they are the <u>most</u> aware. I don't know, never having understood an ant from his point of view. Mosquitoes are born in stagnant ponds and wing into the night looking for blood. Their whining passion – a compulsion.

In fall the rains come slowly at first, then soak the mountainous watershed across the highway. As rains continue into night, the thin topsoil gets saturated and runoff goes twisting and turning, following the arbitrary dictates of gravity, dropping and running in prescribed pathways around stones and boulders and tree roots toward the creek bottom. Moving ever faster it finds the 42 inch diameter, 100 foot long culvert beneath the highway, and runs into the dry creek bed on our property. It carries a multitude of leaves and debris and rousts a few spiders, beetles, ants, and moths, and by the next evening, the rain, a foot deep and five feet across, is striking the red-brown, hoary pockmarked boulders in a roar. The creatures of the creek, no doubt, took refuge on the sloping banks, and climbed, dripping, into holes to out wait the downpour; the storm water, swirling, tumbling, casting crystal reflections, bubbling, pouring, cleaning the creek of debris and otherwise establishing its right and claiming its territory. The mindful creatures accept the normal cycles of their fate and life continues. And what about the Pentachaeta Lyonii, long may she reign? I wish I knew what she looked like.

FLY IN THE ROCKET SHIP
(A story problem)

If there was a fly in the cockpit of a rocket ship, zipping through space at the rate of 9,000 feet-per-second, 120 miles above earth, and it was buzzing around the captain's face, driving him bonkers and he maniacally jammed the stick, full-throttle, lurching the ship forward and doubling the speed once a minute, and the fly, totally unprepared, hurtled wing over eyeball toward the rear of the ship 20 feet away, how many seconds would elapse until the fly whammed into the rear bulkhead and slid to the floor?

A) If he weighed one ounce?
B) If he weighed one half pound?
C) If he weighed 25 pounds?

WHERE HAVE I BEEN?

*Y*eah, I go way back. I was here even *before* 1960. Now, that's old. I just got my name in the *"Twenty-five Years Ago Today"* column of the Malibu Times. I remember the owner-editor, Reeves Templeman, when he was still getting out issues with his wife Eileen. When she died many years later, Reeves scattered her ashes from a light plane into the Pacific off the Malibu coast. I liked Eileen, she was pretty and efficient.

I did houses for Bruce Koch, a likeable plasterer-turned-contractor. I fixed one house that was already started and designed two more for him. One later slipped down the hill. Yes, it was lost in a landslide. I went out one morning to see a D-9 bulldozer with one cable attached to the house's underpinning and another tied around the trunk of a big pine tree to prevent it from crashing 80 feet to the Malibu Cove Colony pavement below.

Shortly thereafter, the second house I designed on the same bluff right next to it, mysteriously burned in the night. I visited the charred remains. Was it done for the insurance? You could get fire insurance then, but they didn't offer slide insurance.

Mario Quiros, the Malibu land surveyor, and I shared an office in the early days. Mario was terrific, honest and salt-of-the-earth kind of guy. If everyone were like Mario, there would be no wars. Mario and his wife, Lavonia, raised three beautiful children in a single room, a former closet no larger than five by seven feet. A triple bunk bed occupied one wall and a small double-hung window the other, with a door to the bathroom beyond. The children turned out the sweetest adults you'd ever want to know.

I knew Joe Schiro, too. Joe, a military man-turned-contractor, was a man of integrity and had the courage of his convictions. I've seen old Joe put himself right on the line testing his intelligence and credibility at Chamber of Commerce meetings and other public functions. Joe often missed the point, as if there were great gaps in his thinking. But he had integrity, and though I thought him wrong some of the time, it didn't matter to me because he listened inwardly, pursued his own ideas, and remained true to himself. He was true to what he believed and I thought this to be admired.

Then I knew Dave Duncan, who along with Art Jones, formed one of the earliest, if not the earliest and most powerful real estate companies in Malibu. Dave, a vigorous man, liked to take mile-long early morning swims in the ocean year-round and well into his 70s. And Art Jones, whom I thought to be unapproachable, self-centered, and crotchety, owned a great many acres of Malibu property and wouldn't sell cheaply to anybody. Later, he took up with a young real estate agent's beautiful wife and lived unmarried with her for many years. I knew the agent, Rudy, who came from Germany and was in agony over the affair, but helpless in doing anything.

I knew fire and floods, too. In the big fire of '56, when I still lived in Santa Monica Canyon, I could see Malibu burning all the way from the Santa Monica bluffs. In the distance beyond the curving coastline, it looked like a Bosch painting of Hell and Damnation. The angry infection growled and seared and blackened the hills with 10,000 feet of thick, black smoke billowing out to sea and helicopters in the forefront, silhouetted like whirling black bugs.

Then came the rains in '69 pounding down on the blackened hills and the floods. I can still hear the rocks at 3:00 AM clattering and tumbling in a silt-laden torrent down Malibu Creek into the Malibu Lagoon and rushing out to sea. The surf break was irreparably changed for years. I've surfed and skin-dived and body-ridden the waves and sailed. I've hiked the mountains, reluctantly killed rattlers on my doorstep for fear they might strike the children, and seen the moon rise, big as a washtub, over Palos Verdes, the ocean, and 23 acres of blooming geraniums, while the blazing orange sun sank over purple Santa Ana wind waves disappearing over Point Dume. Raised my family here, too.

ORANGES

Let's see, the produce department would be in that direction. That's where it's been for three years now. Boy, they never change this place. I'll just roll this basket over to the oranges. Hey! They look pretty good. Let's see, do I want navels or Valencias? The Valencias are a little green looking. Guess I'll take some navels.

I like navels because they're easier to peel. Just bite the top, grab a handful a' skin and rip 'er back. A coupla tears and whammo, you got yourself a peeled orange. I usually rip out the pith. Pith is OK, I guess, not too tasty. Gramma Rucker used to say, *"Eat the pith. It's good for you."* I usually thought, *"Pith on you, Gramma,"* but I'd never say it aloud.

Valencias, though, are another story. Valencias are not bad once you get them peeled. But peeling them. Wow! You ever try to peel a Valencia? It's a tiger! I bite the top just like the navels, but go through the skin and juice squirts on my shirt. *"Son of a gun! This is going to be one messy orange!"* Then I sink my nails in the peel and try to rip 'er back. But, noooo! A little chunk comes off and I've jammed peelings up my fingernails and one is starting to sting and bleed. At this point, I'm deciding do I want this orange or not? The rest of the peel I have to work off in tiny squares, ripped off by my thumb.

By the time I get the darn thing peeled, you'd think I'd run under a juice sprinkler. Prying the orange sections apart is even worse; more juice runs out like a waterfall. I have to jump back and let 'er fall on the rug or tablecloth or chair or whatever. Then the seeds! Valencias are nothin' BUT seeds! Where you goin' to throw 'em? Where you goin' to spit 'em?

When I ride in the car and eat Valencias, I spit the seeds out the window. But, I always worry. Is a police officer going to pull me over and say, *"OK, wise guy! What's with the seeds?"*

"Sorry officer," I say.

And the officer says, *"Don't you know there's a law against open Valencias in the car?"*

"Was that on the test?" I say.

"Don't you know those seeds could fly back and break a windshield, or knock a lady off her scooter, or a motorist, swerving to avoid a bouncing orange seed, could smack a pole?" Says the officer.

"I never thought of it that way, sir," say I.

"I'm letting you off this time, but next time, buy navels," says the officer.

"OK, sir," say I.

"They're easier to eat and have no messy seeds," says the officer.

"Yes sir!" Say I.

Now, that's kind of an exaggerated way to look at things, but you get what I mean.

WE SHALL PREVAIL!

I think the whole idea of a beautiful planet spinning all alone in a black void is a brutal, ruthless idea! And in four billion years, the planet Earth has managed to get a thin ozone layer of gas that protects all that lives on the surface; plants, animals, fish, reptiles, insects, birds, man, and everything else. There are millions and billions and trillions of stars in the universe. In the center of the galaxies, word has it, there are black holes where a teaspoonful of black hole matter weighs more than ten thousand suns. Other stars explode, comets glide endlessly through eternity, and our planet, our precious little, watery planet, spins on its axis with its thin, gaseous ozone, and huge orbiting moon, both rotating around an average, but oh-so-important sun.

So, what if our sun blows up? Happens all the time. I can imagine an intelligent being far away on another planet who <u>knows</u> how many planets there are. He knows they surround us by the zillions *(true, they are light years away)* but, there, on the interstellar news he hears that one planet, Earth, blew itself up a half-hour ago. No survivors. *(Probably hearing this just after a soap commercial.)* But of course he knows there are many planets in the universe dying all the time. Big deal! He knows it's doubtful there will be an overpopulation of stars or planets, for the universe is self-regulating; there being a finite amount of matter coming and going. If one section of the universe gets overcrowded, stars fall into each other and explode into gas that forms galaxies and solar systems, or they implode and form black holes. He knows the quest of the universe is for stability, dependability and growth, as well as wildness, life and death.

Do I think the pieces of earth *(and fragments of arms and legs)* are lost and gone forever? No, sir! They are temporarily out in the cold *(-270 degrees Centigrade)* and eventually will wind up as part of something else. One planet blowing up in a billion quadrillion makes little difference.

But, says another, what if our beautiful planet is the <u>only</u> one among all the stars we see through our telescopes. *(By the way, there are so many stars to be seen through one view of even the simplest telescopes they look like dense fog.)* There is an *INCONCEIVABLE* number of stars out there. Yes, folks, it's a starry gas out there.

Now supposing we live on the *only* planet in the universal gas or stars we see on a clear night. I ask you, to have something <u>this</u> beautiful and <u>this</u> rare to use and enjoy all at the same time makes losing it *REAL* poignant. I'd be *SO* sorry, folks, you can't believe it.

Finally, this universal starry gas from other stars' explosions makes Earth a beautiful life-supporting planet and gives it a thin atmosphere that protects and enables all life. Then one species, man, *(in some ways the idiot-species of all time)* makes a bomb to blow up all living creatures including us. But, this intellectually over-developed man is capable of miracles, too, because he/she can discover DNA, make rocket ships that go to Mars and eliminate disease, while at the same time inventing bombs to blow up the planet.

If I was God and had decided on a *"hands off policy,"* and wanted to play observer and just see what *"man"* would do, I'd speculate three things: *(1)* He'll blow it up. *(2)* He'll make the planet awfully sick. *(3)* He'll opt for his own and the planet's life and not blow it up and pull a *"save."*

Of course, I'm not God. If I were, I'd slap *"man"* up the side of the head and tell him, *"Get it together!"* But then I wonder, why is man <u>not</u> together? Why does man, being part God himself, seem not to be in control of himself? Then, I look around and see that most everything is *NOT* in control of itself. I cleaned up a mess of ants on the sink yesterday. The ants had no control over their instinct to hunt for food in my sink. Agent Orange defoliated the Vietnam trees and after the war exposed people were mortally affected. Trees and people had no control in Vietnam. In India, 2,000 people suddenly died because poison gas mysteriously leaked from the Earth. The victims had no control.

Eventually I came to the conclusion that *"man,"* as we

know him, cannot control himself or much of anything. I've looked back in history for a time when he <u>did</u> control himself and have discovered he <u>never</u> controlled himself. He never controlled his anger, greed, revenge or amount of education, and as long as *"man"* is here, the planet will be infested with *man's* disease.

Of course, the U. S. <u>did</u> send wheat to Africa, and we do seem to be a freer people than in the past, and brilliant people <u>do</u> win the Nobel Peace Prize. What the world needs is a paradigm shift. Let us pray.

TOAST AND TWIRL

I don't know exactly why I like to toast and twirl, but I do. Especially on Sunday morning when Marge and my number three daughter, Amanda, are around. They will be cutting fruit and fixing pancakes in the kitchen, which is one step away from the living room. I'll be wearing sweat clothes watching cartoons on the TV. I sleep in my sweat pants and T-shirt. I am just putting some toast in the toaster when I get this great urge to twirl.

I can twirl both ways, left or right. I learned it in a movement class I was in a while ago. I don't twirl on my toes like Baryshnikov. I twirl on my heels. I stick out my leg, the one opposite my twirling leg, and swing it powerfully around, which sets off the twirling. Most of the time, when I finish the twirl, I'm off balance and have to catch myself with my spinning leg. Marge and Amanda both admit that my rather feathery hair flies straight out during the twirl. I still can't twirl and stay on balance every time and have lots of practicing to do before I get it right.

Yet every now and then I will twirl once around and stay perfectly on balance. When I do this, I break into a big grin because it feels so good and I am making progress.

Marge and Amanda frequently say, *"There he goes again."* Sometimes I twirl without toasting. I'll just twirl to the cartoons. The cartoons are blowing up and zapping each other with ray guns, and big mechanical monsters are marching invincibly down on all-too-human heroes. It's then I catch glimpses of two heads peering secretively from the kitchen and overhear whispering. *"Marge, he's doing it again."*

Viveka, my number one daughter, thinks Marge, Amanda and I need neighbors so we'll have role models and know how to conduct ourselves in civilized America. Marge thinks she's so superior, though. She tolerates me quietly while I twirl. But I want to tell you this, one time I came suddenly from the kitchen to the bedroom and there she was, in her pajamas, dancing on the bed! I said, *"Marge, what are you doing?"*

She just laughed and said, *"Dancing."* I guess she felt she didn't have to apologize for the likes of me. Of course, if I do living room twirls, I guess I can't complain about bedroom dancing.

Now, so you won't think Marge and I are the only ones hopelessly weird, let me tell you about Amanda, who is not entirely blameless. She's a living room sleeper. She only sleeps when there's commotion. She usually sleeps under the afghan my mother crocheted that's a little short, so she has to tuck her legs up in order to get completely under. I slam doors, flush toilets, run the disposal, play the radio, talk on the telephone, have guests, and practice bongos. Or I let Romeo, her dog, romp and growl next to her couch with the neighborhood dogs, Fatsy-Patsy and Chelsea. I shout to them, *"Outside! Outside!"* and the noisier it is, the sounder she sleeps.

I've seen her get up, let the dog out, flop back on the couch and never wake up. We could celebrate the 4th of July and New Year's Eve while she's napping without disturbing her whatsoever! Knowing she sleeps so soundly and seizing the afternoon opportunity, Marge being in her separate studio, I'll stick some toast in the toaster, turn on Three's Company and practice a few twirls. Sometimes Romeo barks at me, but most of the time he sleeps, his temperament being somewhat like that of Amanda's. After that I lie down in a fit of exhaustion, or sit at my desk and draw a few cartoons.

Viveka came in a day or so ago, and caught Amanda studying for her logic exam at the dining table and me drafting on my home board. She asked, *"What are you doing, taking a work break?"*

I think I do my best twirling while toasting. There's something about waiting for the toast to be done and not wasting time but doing something soul satisfying to improve oneself. It makes the toasting go faster, too. Twirl and toast, toast and twirl, then sit right down for a good old Sunday breakfast with your family and have a good day. Twirl and toast, toast and twirl. Try it, you'll like it.

TRUTH AND BEAUTY

*L*et's talk about Truth and Beauty for a moment. Now, I know other philosophers and great men have talked about Truth and Beauty before this. I'm not so self-important that I think I'm the first one to talk about such an important and significant subject as Truth and Beauty. Actually, Truth and Beauty is not really one subject. Some of you have covered this. No, Truth and Beauty are really two subjects. *(1)* Truth, and *(2)* Beauty. For purposes of this essay and to save time, I will consider both at the same time.

I ask myself, what object or idea has both characteristics of Truth and Beauty at the same time? Right off, what comes to mind is a peanut butter sandwich. The Truth being in its nourishment and the Beauty in the rich, whole wheat color of the bread, tantalizingly enfolding the rich, creamy, golden-brown peanut butter. I can smell that sandwich right now with every fiber of my being.

Or take a rose. Obviously, a rose has qualities of Beauty. Think about a bouquet of roses, let's say, on the dining room table. Beautiful, wouldn't you say? But where is the Truth? Roses have no Truth, lest it be in their Beauty. Show me a man who does not think roses are pretty and I'll show you a <u>liar</u>!

Yes, roses have universal appeal. Speaking of appeal, apples are a fine example of Truth and Beauty combined. Or hamburgers, or pecan pie with rich, Cool Whip on it, or whipped cream with strawberries, or a thick, red, tender piece of fried liver, peeking out from a bed of juicy onions, nourishing and radiantly beautiful. Foods are a fine example of Truth and Beauty. I'm so hungry right now, I could eat a Bonus Jack.

Actually, I'm bored with the subject of Truth and Beauty. There's nothing much more to say about it anyway. Everything has some kind of Truth and some kind of Beauty. Maybe dog poo-poo is a little lacking in Beauty, but certainly has a lot of Truth. There's no denying dog poo-poo if it's on your shoe when you're in the car going to a wedding. Or, how about a plate of worms? That's certainly a lot of Truth in one gooey mass with no Beauty, unless you're a robin. And worms, you know, have no knowledge of Beauty. They can't even see, right?

So, where does that leave us? It's obvious to me why the subject of Truth and Beauty is only thought of by the smartest of us. It's because it takes a genius to figure out what to say about it. At first glance, it may appear, *"You've seen one Truth and Beauty, you've seen 'em all!"* But this essay proves there is more to Truth and Beauty than meets the eye.

How many words have I got to go, Pete? I've about exhausted the subject. Guess I can pad out the rest of this essay by writing a big, *"HI TO MOM!" Howdy, uncle Ralph! See you in Des Moines on the Fourth. Thinking about YOU, brother Dave. Love to Marge and the kids!"*

CLOSE CALL

Marge and I love to hike. One early Sunday morning we took an hour's climb to the top of a mountain ridge on the other side of a sweeping natural valley. It was marvelous ascending along the narrow, dirt Jeep trail. At the top we tarried, sitting on a boulder in the breeze, absorbing the sun and the early atmosphere. A little drowsy, we dozed, and later, when the sun was higher, we awoke. Time to descend, but not by the same route we'd arrived. Oh, no. We'd skirt the meadow on the mountain's backside, go up through the rock pass and back down the steep face of the mountain by the narrow footpath. I'd been there before. But how could I have known what was about to happen?

"Are you sure you know the way?" Marge asked.

"Trust me!" I replied.

Down the back trail we went, brush high overhead. Occasionally we caught glimpses of the backside valley through the bushes and beyond, and the muted ridges of hazy blue mountains. It was darker on the north side of the mountain, and wetter, too. We made our way around several puddles that had made the trail mucky and unpleasant for walking.

"This doesn't seem the right way." Marge complained.

"I've been this way before." I said. *"I know where it leads."*

We hiked down the rutted trail, Marge picking her way around the slippery stones. Soon we would reach the meadow. Little did I know what was shortly to come. *"There's the meadow, Marge!"* I said. Then I looked again and stopped awestruck!

Marge, noticing my petrified stance, reached my side and asked, *"What is it?"*

Then, she saw it, too! A full-grown cow, brown and white, was standing in the path, not a hundred feet away, motionless, alert and gazing at us intensively. Marge resumed walking. I whispered hoarsely, *"Marge, where are you going?" Are you crazy? There's a cow directly in our path!"*

"I know." Marge said, and kept on walking.

Then I noticed other cows. *"Marge! There's other cows!"* I cried.

We had inadvertently stumbled on a private group of meadow cows. Marge continued her pace. I moved cautiously after her.

"We are in a whole group of meadow cows!" I called out.

There must have been four or five of these menacing beasts spread out in the meadow, one under a tree, two in full sun, and one standing half in the bushes. Here and there, they were, all looking at us and one huge cow standing defiantly in front of us in the middle of our only path.

Thinking back, that cow could probably have overtaken us with a single bound from its powerful hind muscles. I started to go WAY around the angry cow, but my foot sank deep in the spongy grass. Suddenly, the cow turned on us, and ran away from us another one hundred feet down the path, tail flying. Then it stood still, flicking its ears and looking directly in our eyes. Boy, was that cow mad!

"Marge! I said, *"Maybe we should go back the way we came."*

Marge continued along the path toward the cow. I followed well behind. The other cows continued watching us, too. Every one of them had stopped munching on the grassy meadow and was staring straight at us. We didn't dare make a false move! You could have heard a pin drop. Each of those cows must have outweighed us ten or twelve times. One false move and we would have been cow meat! I could see headlines: *"BONES OF COUPLE FOUND MANGLED BY UNTENDED MEADOW COWS."*

Marge shooed the cow off the path and we walked briskly out of that meadow. I took the lead, boldly marching up the trail I now recognized as the one I'd traveled before. We made it, but that was one unexpected adventure that was just too close for comfort. It was what I'd call a *CLOSE CALL!*

DAVID AND MYRA

I walked out of the apartment angry as hell! The rain beat on my forehead and splashed on my knees. It was imperative I get my thoughts in order. What had happened was all too shocking; walking the streets, cars zooming everywhere, people scrambling to who-knows-where. It was all so new. What could I do? To whom could I turn?

I decided to walk to the East Bridge, across to 44th and then the remaining block to DiAngelo's for a drink. Maybe tying one on would settle my nerves. The rain bit sharply into the backs of my hands and stung my ears. I pulled the collar of Walt's mohair coat more securely around my throat. The night rain was turning to sleet. It was bitterly cold.

Just as well! Perhaps I deserved it. The bridge loomed dimly in the stinging drizzle. There was a dark female shape under the street lamp. Whoever it was wore a black coat and a black hat that covered her face. She was staring into the black choppy river whipped by the night wind sixty feet below. Another stride would have taken me past her except that I heard my name spoken softly and clearly. *"David."* The word etched itself into my mind, and I stopped and peered into the darkness of her face. She turned, removing her hat.

Her full, rich hair tumbled to her shoulders. *"Myra? What are you doing here?"* My words were coarse and seemed to come from another body.

"Waiting for you," she said, letting both hands drop to her sides in a gesture of helplessness.

"How did you know I'd be passing this way?" I spoke through clenched teeth. The sleet covered her hair and shoulders with a soft, white crust.

"I know you, David. I knew you'd be walking after the apartment experience." She replaced her hat, smoothing her hair fetchingly.

"How did you know about that?" I shoved my hands deep into the pockets of my coat, hunched my shoulders, shivered and exhaled mist.

"I was with you … Oh, I wasn't actually there. I was having tea, alone, when a cold chill seized me. Spasms convulsed my body. I felt your presence and knew something of great importance was happening to you." She moved closer.

I took her fragile hands in my own. They were like trembling old chicken-bones. *"You sensed my mortification, my disbelief, the incomprehensible catastrophe?"* She looked deeply into my eyes for one eternal moment, searching ... searching.

"Yes." She spoke assertively. A flood of feelings rippled down my spine, through my stomach and out my toes.

"How could she have known?" I thought.

"Why don't you tell me about it," Myra asked, clasping both my hands, her eyes sympathetic, compelling.

"My … my …" I choked. *"My choo-choo train derailed."* I burst into tears.

"There, there, David," said Myra, holding me close.

ROMEO

When I returned to my studio this morning, I suddenly opened the door, and there was Romeo sitting on my drafting stool, whirling 'round and 'round. I'd left him to finish up some drafting, but there he was, whirling on my stool and diddling with my electric eraser. I said, *"Off My Stool!"* He slunk under the conference table and tried to avoid my gaze. He's a pretty smart dog, though, on the whole, except for his spelling.

I left him to rake the decomposed granite the other day, you know, like a Japanese garden. When I returned it was only half-raked and the other half looked like neighborhood dogs were scuffling. I scolded him, grabbed the rake and said, *"Here! This is how you do it. Long, even strokes. See! Now you try it!"* I told him to practice while I went in to get some brownies. I guess he's coming along, but sometimes it seems mighty slow.

"Perhaps we're expecting too much of him," said my daughter, Amanda.

"Perhaps so," I said.

I told him to wash his doggy dish, too. Never does. I came back. There were suds and water all over the floor, soap in his half-cleaned bowl and Romeo a wet mess, giving me a *"Ha! Ha! Ha! Sorry!"* Grin. I slammed the water shut and told him to go play with Chelsea and her dog-son, Fatsy-Patsy. He went out right away. Soon, he and Chelsea and Fatsy-Patsy were running and jumping all over each other, messing up my half-raked, decomposed granite Japanese garden, lawn and motor court.

Sometimes, another dog with white eyes comes over. He's the type of dog that gives you eye contact, which is worrisome, particularly with his white eyes. I've named him, Al, for lack of knowing his real name. Romeo has it IN for Al. No way is Al going to invade Romeo's territory and tinkle all over the concrete block walls, the plants and the corner of the house.

With a whine and a grunt and the sound of powerful claws digging into the dirt, Romeo, at the speed of light, bounds after the white-eyed intruder until, with the bumping and swaying of a distant bush, it's over!

Romeo returns, tongue out, panting, and having done his duty, happily re-establishes his territory in the usual way.

Neither dog realizes it is MY territory and those are MY block walls, MY plants and MY corner of the house. It takes a week for the drooping flowers to perk up.

Well, here's Romeo again. He wants a pat on the head and a snack. I tell him to forget it. Now he's whining to get out and I've got to push my chair WAY back, get up, walk WAY across the room, turn the door handle WAY around and let him out. I decide. *"No way! You are going to sit up at that computer to do my books!"*

Romeo's pretty good at math, though. He knows addition and subtraction, but his multiplication stinks. I checked him out one day last week. He had 9x6 = 57. I had to straighten him out. GOD! Here's Fatsy-Patsy, the neighborhood dog, again. *"Romeo! OUT!"*

When Romeo wants to go out, he stands by the door and locks my eyes with his and goes, *"Mnnng! Mnnng! Mnnng!"* I let him in. I let him out. Usually Amanda takes him with her wherever she goes in the car. Romeo jumps into the front seat, sits upright and stares out the front window from the passenger seat like a person. I've advised Amanda to get the dog sunglasses, but she hasn't done it yet. You can get dog sunglasses, I think, at the pet store.

Returning from lunch, I noticed Romeo was at the computer. I checked the screen to see what he was writing. I saw about 40,000 O's. Romeo looked at me. I looked at him. I said, *"Romeo! Get your paw off the O!"* He lifted his paw and gave an expression as if to say, *"Oops! Ha! Ha! Ha!"* He always loses his DOS manual, too. And, you should see it when it does turn up. It's got paw marks all over the pages, the covers are ripped off; it's folded and torn. A real mess! He loves it, though.

You'd think a healthy, outdoor dog like Romeo would read some of the more popular books and magazines for dogs, like <u>Lassie Bites a Bear</u> or <u>Rin-Tin-Tin Goes Garbage Hopping</u> or <u>Playdog.</u> But, noooo! He likes his DOS manual.

If he were human, he'd work for Litton Industries or be in the space program. I keep telling him if he keeps up all this book and computer stuff, he's going to ruin his eyes. He doesn't listen to me, though.

One day I found him lying on his back reading the DOS manual with his legs crossed. I tell him it's bad for his eyes. I explained what my mother told me, *"When you read lying down, your bent neck restricts blood flow to the brain."* He promises he's going to sit up straight, but never does. I don't know why Amanda's not more strict with him.

One day Amanda came home. I was drafting, and Romeo was lying with his head on his paws gathering strength for imagined activities. I asked Amanda if she'd seen the DOS manual.

She said, *"No! I haven't seen it lately."*

"The last time I saw it," I said, *"it was beat up. Ripped to shreds!"* I told him, *"Don't bury it any more! Nobody's going to take it!"* I told Amanda, *"The reason we haven't seen his DOS manual is because it's buried!"*

NINETY-POUND HECTOR AND THE GRASSY SLOPE
(A Story Problem)

*I*f 90 pound Hector, who has a belt-line girth of 36 inches, lies on his side at the top of a 30 foot hill in the park, and showing off, rolls sideways, over and over, down a steep grassy slope, a pink and red blur of arms, legs, flying hair, loose change and untied shoelaces. How many revolutions would he make before falling off the low bank into the creek at the bottom of the hill?

A) If he did not throw up?

B) If he threw up two-thirds of the way down, shrinking his girth size to 30 inches?

COWS AT CALAMIGOS

At 6:30 this chilly winter morning, dressed in sweats and gym shoes, I was out for my daily 45 minute run-walk, and decided to come back through Calamigos Ranch. I dropped down the hill through the dirt parking lot and down one of the pathways leading through an oak grove. I zipped past the big barn they use for large dances, then diagonally across the green grass toward the row of large mulberry trees. I slowed to a stroll to catch my breath, and enjoyed the brisk, fresh air and shaded view of the creek as I clumped across the bridge toward the animal pen.

Calamigos ranch has a petting zoo during the summer consisting of eight or ten sheep, the same number of goats of various sizes and ages, and one calf. The baby cow, a black and white Holstein, I believe, was special, because, though about the same size as the larger sheep, it could easily be explained as another kind of animal to the delighted visiting children.

During the past two years, however, the cow has grown almost to full size and the owners, having compassion for the cows apparent loneliness, acquired another Holstein about the same sex, size and age to keep it company. Now they have two cows.

This morning I found them separated from the sheep and goats by a low fence, although one sheep was in with them. I don't know why the single sheep was with them. Perhaps it had been a bad sheep and was being isolated from its kind. Perhaps it snuck in because it really liked cows, or was a sheep in heat. I don't know why the sheep was in with the cows. The sheep isn't part of this story anyway. Moving on.

I have never been comfortable around large farm animals, but since I was separated from what I considered to be cows of good breeding by a swampy area of twenty feet and an elbow-high fence, and was almost done with my run anyway, and needed a breather, I thought it would be a good time to put my foot on the rail and satisfy my curiosity with a good look. Get to know cows!

The cows, one facing me head-on, the other facing away with its head turned toward me, both froze in their tracks. The one facing me stopped chewing and was motionless. The other, also frighteningly stationary, looked at me and continued chewing. Cud, as I remember.

Eyes of cows are basically on the sides of their heads, and when the one facing me stared at me, all I could see was two little vertical slits, flanked by long eyelashes sticking out sideways. I wondered if he got a full view of me. I understand from Marge, who told me later, that cows and horses have horizontal pupils that allow them to see almost 360 degrees. However, they do have a blind spot directly behind them, in the vicinity of their tail. She says you should never sneak up behind a cow, because they instinctively kick at whatever they can't see and you might find yourself in the dust, on the ground with a major injury you can't yet feel. Moving on.

Cows are herbivorous, that is, they only eat vegetable matter, so theoretically, since I am an animal, they wouldn't eat me. Therefore, I have nothing to worry about when it comes to cows. I could even feed them dandelions or other weeds. They might even like it. However, in so doing, if my hand were too close, let's say my drafting hand, and they wanted to snip off a few dandelions, might they not snip off a couple of my fingers as well? Of course, not liking meat, they would probably spit them out and continue chewing. I can see them lying, mangled, in the dirt. It's not a pretty picture. Of course, I would be at the loss, my drafting hand and all, but I couldn't blame them, now, could I? Really!

I don't know if cows are subject to passion or wild fits of sudden anger. Bulls get hysterical if you show them red. What's the color of my shirt right now? <u>Not red</u>, OK! Do cows get mad if you stare at them, like I'm doing right now? How high can cows leap? Could they leap over this fence and chase me down the path? It doesn't sound reasonable.

OH! Here comes one to see me. He ... she probably thinks I've got a treat for her, like a piece of corn or a carrot. As if I would be jogging around with cow food. She's striding toward me right through that mucky stuff without a thought. Now the other's coming over, too. I'll steel my nerve and hold my ground. I'm not afraid of Holsteins.

That's not so bad. See, I'm petting its head. I'll just rub the forehead above the place where there looks like there once were horns. Question: Did they remove the horns? Are they too young to have horns? Do girl cows get horns? In any case, it would be judicious if I don't pet the horns. If you pet the horns it makes them squirrelly and they're liable to lose control of their emotions and try to gore you out of the park with their head.

She's sticking her head through the fence. Is she going to lick my stomach? Wouldn't that be a nice cow if she stuck her head through the fence and licked my stomach? What if it's just a trick? She's trying to lure me into a false sense of security and during an unsuspecting moment, rip my guts out. You can't trust cows. I can feel those icy teeth rip into my fresh skin, the blood spurting as I try to run. Then she would crush the fence with her mad strength and begin chasing me home, me bleeding, in pain with a crazed cow who's had its horns scratched, chasing me at full gallop, her friend close behind.

Newspaper headlines: *"Cows Jump Fence, Maim Bystander"* – *"Cows Get Revenge, Trample Onlooker!"* – *"Mad Cows Lose Control, Bite Hand that Feeds Them!"*

What's this? The cow's tongue is coming out, and then going in. She's trying to lick me? I think the cow's name is Georgia.

Anyway, it's time for me to be running along. I don't have any corn anyway. It's unkind to tempt them and not deliver. Must get on with my workday.

POWER OF THE POINT

*I*magine a pointed line ⟶ commonly called an arrow, which for our purpose indicates a direction toward or away from something. The arrow, or pointed line, is a symbol that indicates left, right, up, down, or infinite directions. *The point is the line's <u>reason</u>. The point is the <u>power</u> added to the line.* The pointed line need not be always straight, but can indicate swirling, curving, swooping, diving or any imagined motion through space.

For example, a pointed line can show the delicate, arch of a tracer-bullet traveling a two mile course aimed at a bulls-eye, or a tumbling asteroid on a billion-year elliptical orbit through cold, dark matter, perhaps to indicate relentless forces and the indestructible dynamism of uncontrolled nature.

A pointed line questions or answers *"What"* or *"Where"* and it's always used to highlight an item or idea. If I'm writing, "Doug Rucker makes *so and so,*" it's not as important as if I write" ⟶ Doug Rucker ⟵ " followed by whatever rapturous phrase I can think of. In fact, anything I name or draw gains additional importance when a line with an arrowhead is pointed to it.

A thin, anemic looking arrow is not as strong as a thick, black, arrow. In fact arrows, or pointed lines, can have character. You might say, as all living things *(except some humans)* do, an arrow can have integrity. Each pointed line must carry the importance intended. Drawing any arrow, I must be careful <u>how</u> I draw it.

A pointed line can be imagined small, the size of a bean, or even smaller, the size of a pinhead, or smaller to indicate the direction of an atom, or neutron, or lots of arrows showing the orbits of a swarm of electrons. That, of course, challenges the imagination, since electrons move at unbelievable speeds in arbitrary directions and only the *probability* of their locations can be determined; kind of like trying to point your finger at Reggie Bush or Michael Vick dodging football players.

If I try, I can imagine a group of pointed lines zooming through the atmosphere, showing wind currents of a hurricane, or vertical, wiggly, pointing lines moving down to indicate the plunging direction of a calving Alaskan glacier, or lines showing the protective presence of fog isolating the Sargasso Sea, or a whale diving to the ocean's abysmal plain, or the direction of an alien space ship circling the planet, or an individual, fitted in his powered spacesuit, rocketing lonely and ambivalent, to the moon. *(Let's not eat on the moon tonight. No atmosphere.)*

Pointed lines can be imagined fifty yards long and ten feet wide painted to show 747's where to land, or frantic lines dug deep in the sand by some forlorn being spelling,

"Help!" or a swarm of pointed lines indicating the direction of a flock of birds flying south for the winter, or the erratic motion of bees determinedly moving their queen, or the assumed direction of a rolling, bouncing SUV tumbling over a cliff to smash in a brilliant explosion, or the direction of falling rain as it's acted upon by updrafts in a powerful thunderhead, or stage directions showing movements and marks for actors to stand on and deliver their lines, or a hundred-foot-thick block of wood, tall as the Empire State Building, with a powerful wooden arrowhead painted black pointing to the origin of the big bang.

Clocks have arrows pointing to the time of day, like London's Big Ben, or those on the classroom wall that slowly tick and jump, or thousands of watches on thousands of wrists on thousands of people on thousands of cruises that are depended upon for eating time, reading time, nap time, dancing time, show time, bedtime, with all their hands pointing this way and that.

Arrows, or points on a line, indicate for or against, to or fro, positive or negative. We are all familiar with *2 < 4*, meaning two is less than four, or *4 > 2*, meaning four is greater than two. The point, with no line connected, is a shortened version meaning the same thing. If I say *"Doug > Dave,"* brother Dave might counter with, "No! *Dave > Doug."* You see how it works.

An historian can indicate the direction of human migration across the Bering Strait, the prehistoric motions of continents in their closing or separating, the annual movement of geese, or elephants, or wolves, the world's air currents, the Earth's rotation, or information entering or leaving the brain.

An arrow might be drawn to mark the meta-message of a poem, or the point of a philosophical treatise, or the point of a piece of architecture. For the question, *"What is the artist really trying to say here?"* The answer could be in the form of an arrowhead that would point to the section showing what the artist meant. In fact, anything in the known universe can be indicated and given more or less importance by the simple pointed line.

What's that? You ask, what is the point of this essay? Well … uh … I guess I'd have to make a line with an arrowhead pointing to the title:

$\longrightarrow$ *THE POWER OF THE POINT* $\longleftarrow$

GRIM TALES OF FROG HISTORY

They're only a half-inch long and like us, have arms, legs, eyes, hands and feet and can jump in excess of three inches. They're generally optimistic and think they'll live a long time. Don't add to their disappointment by stepping on them or you might face the following consequences!

A century ago, a California hermit was found lying face-up next to his pond having been trampled to death by thousands of tiny frogs. In fact, because of a superb cover-up, by either Ralph Waldo Emerson or the United States Government, it's hardly known that Henry David Thoreau died the same way when one night thousands of tiny frogs slipped out of Walden Pond and attacked him in three waves; two pincer movements and a clean-up battalion. His mangled body was found with severe webbed foot marks on his face and legs. Beware of tiny frogs, and don't camp near ponds after heavy spring rains, so you won't be listed in: _Grim Tales of Frog History_.

DANCE TO DO

*D*eb, our improvisational dance teacher, asked us to think about new dances we'd like to do. Well, I'd like to do my falling-off-the-bench dance like Arte Johnson used to do on Laugh-In. I'd wear this big coat and bowler hat, carry a cane, and after I tried to pick up an elderly lady, she'd whack me with her purse until I'd fall off the end of the bench in the fetal position and lie there motionless.

Or, I'd like to do my chimp imitation. Scratch my sides, waddle around, pick my nose and go "Hoo! Hoo!" Been done? Oh, well! How about my Gene Kelly sailor dance routine? 'Course, I don't know how to dance that way. Or how about my ripening apple dance? I sit curled in a ball on the bench all sour-puss, then over a five-minute period, I slowly grin, and for the big finish, break into a big, toothy smile and drop off the chair, ripe. Oh, well! How about I dance as a tree? I could get this big live-oak costume and have a fan blow my leaves. Somebody could work sheet metal for thunder sound effects, and I could dance as a tree in a violent rainstorm under a sprinkler hose. For the finale, I get hit by lightning. Too much work?

How about this? I do my sword dance with broom

handles, taking both parts. I parry and thrust, and leaping over to assume an imaginary opponent, charge in a flurry of slashing movements, then leaping over to assume my former role, I duel with myself. Get it? Boring? How about my bunny dance routine? I get this huge, furry rabbit costume with floppy ears, bugs bunny teeth and snow-bunny tail, and hop around tossing carrots from a bag into the audience.

Or how about my *"Singin' in the Rain"* dance under a hose? I know. Gets the floor soaked. Get this! I put on chain mail, wear some bust balloons and come as Joan of Arc.

"This is a dance performance, not a costume party!"

How about I act the part of the frog prince in the ballet, Giselle? We get nineteen dumb fairies with white tutus and one smart fairy dressed in a blue tutu. We dance around, and then she throws me in the lake.

"We can't afford a cast of thousands."

Well, here I am, bustin' my you-know-what trying to come up with some good dances and you're shooting them down.

"You call these dances?" Sounds more like a twenty-five-year movie review."

How about my bowling ball dance? Dirk, Ron and Skylar can be the pins. I roll at them doing somersaults and knock them over every which-ways.

"Mmmmm! Not bad. We'll keep that one for now."

Another dance would be my James Cagney gangster

dance I do with a wooden Tommy gun. I murder the audience.

"A little too hostile, don't you think?"

OK. How about I put on my Gabby Hayes look-alike costume, turn up my hat brim, clunk around in my spurs, chaw tobacco and spit?

"Not original or sanitary."

How's this? I wear my Norbert Nerd hat and high-water pants with a bag of golf clubs and hit a few balls into anyone that might come?

"Too dangerous."

Boy, are you tough. How about I get a mask and some silver bullets. You come as Tonto and I.....

PIE CRUST

*L*ast month, I made a health food apple pie. That means no sugar, no salt. I used dates over the apples as a sweetener. I made my own crust from scratch. You know, flour, shortening and water; make it into a dough ball and roll it with a rolling pin?

Well, the recipe only called for five teaspoons full of water. The less water, the lighter and flakier the crust. But five teaspoons didn't do any good. Ten didn't do any good, either. The dough kept sticking to the rolling pin, which really made me mad. I had to do it over and over, adding more and more water, and it was still sticking, until eventually, I must have put five glasses of water in that dough before I could get it to roll out without sticking like its supposed to. I pounded that son-of-a ding-dong! Man! Was I ticked!

I said to myself, I'll get you *(swear word)*, and beat it with my fist and squeezed it in a ball and pounded it on the bread board. But, I got it! Pretty soon, it learned who was boss! I got that dough ball all thick and gluey, and rolled it out, limp and thin, and put it above and below the apple-date filling and edge-trimmed it with a knife like cooks do on TV. Then I baked it to perfection, and that pie crust was crunchy, like taco shells, and pretty good, too. But, I tell you, for a while, that pie crust ticked me off!

NOVOCAINE

*T*he dentist is really a trip. I get off on the novocaine and when I get out of the office, I go on a buying spree. All I want to do is buy something. I come out in the bright morning sun with a numb jaw and all I can think of is, *"Buy! Buy! Buy!"* I get in my car, slam the door, and take off for the nearest store.

I usually buy records or books or stationery. Actually, I'd love to eat, too, but you gotta wait an hour or so before you can bite down. This time I went to the Melody Music Store in Pacific Palisades.

I browsed for a few minutes then I saw this harmonica. I had always wanted a harmonica since I was a kid about a half-century ago. This one looked swell. You can always get those cheapo ones, I thought, but they don't have enough octaves, they're usually out of tune and definitely not chromatic. This harmonica looked perfect. It had halftones and two-and-a-half octaves, but it was too expensive at $45. I turned it over in my hands a couple of times. *"Heck! I'm worth it,"* I said to myself. Wasn't I good? Didn't I suffer pain in the dentist's office? What's $45, anyway? I can afford it. 'Course, the salesman pointed out the vast difference between the $45 harmonicas and the only $85 one he had in the store. He took it out of the glass case. It was a chromatic Hohner with four complete octaves and a beauty. It felt good in my hands.

I really wanted that Hohner. Beads of perspiration formed on my cold forehead. After all, I reasoned, this would be a lifetime harmonica. When you think of having your lifetime harmonica needs met once and for all for only $85, well, wouldn't it be a good idea? My harmonica needs would be over.

In a strangely unfamiliar voice, I heard myself say, *"I'll take it."* I wrote out a check in a daze, and walked out with the heavy little instrument in the Melody Store plastic bag with the sales slip.

The salesman was quite sure I had made the right choice. As it turned out, I played that $85 harmonica a lot. 'Course, I never told anybody how much I paid for it. I kept it in the glove compartment for three years and played it while I was driving on the road. I was kind of a closet harmonica player.

But, I've got this front tooth that sticks out in front of the rest. Turns out my lip hurts when I play too much. My career never had a chance. The world would have been saddened had it ever found out what it missed, so I've kept it a secret 'til now. So much for novocaine and *"Buy! Buy! Buy!"*

LEFT BRAIN – RIGHT BRAIN

*T*his morning, I showered and dressed for work. Had to supervise a couple of jobs. It's maybe 8:00 AM and I'm getting on with the day because I have things to do here later. So I whip my heavy protein drink in the blender, put it in the plastic container with the easy-drink lid, and set it out with notebook on the drafting table ready to go. I lock the back door and I'm going off, right? Gonna drink my breakfast in the car on the way, right? Wrong! I can't find my keys.

I go out to the car to see if I left them there. Nope, not in the ignition, not in the trunk lid, not on the seat, not in the car, too bad. So, I look through my junk drawer where I usually keep them. Not there. Then I look to see if they coulda fallen outta my pockets when I put my pants on the hanger. Maybe they fell in my shoes. I turn all three pair upside down and shake 'em. I go through my shirt and jacket pockets. Nothing.

Then, I'm playing *"warmer-colder"* with myself. When we were kids, Dad would hide something in the room for us to find and if we were moving closer to it he would say *"warmer,"* and if farther, he'd say *"colder."* Sometimes he'd say, *"You're so far from it, you're frozen!"* or, *"You're at the North Pole!"* or, *"You're an icicle!"* Things like that. Or, *"You're so close you're burning up! If it was a snake, it would have bit you by now!"* Things like that.

So, I'm playing *"warmer-colder"* with myself inside my closet feeling like an idiot because I've got things to do, places to go, and I'm all dressed up and my drink is warming and the day is wasting. Then, while drinking my breakfast in the kitchen, I decide to pull a *"Mammy Yokum"*, that is, mark a bloody *"X"* on my forehead, whirl three times and fall to the floor in a trance where a vision will show me where I left my car keys.

Leaving out the blood and whirling part, I lay down on the bed, flat on my back in the yoga *"Death Pose."* I close my eyes and try to visualize where I left the keys. *"Let's see, last night I came home …"*

I lay there for five minutes, seven minutes, ten minutes … I'm getting sleepy. The Mammy Yokum technique is not happening. Exasperated, I leap from the bed. *"Heck, I'll use the old left-hand writing technique. I'll ask my left hand where the keys are."*

The left hand, being controlled by the right brain, the nerve center for feelings, hunches, and intuition; the silent observer and recorder of every action from birth to death, should know where the keys are. I have tried using my left brain, the half responsible for reasoning, languages, mathematics, and cold logic, without success. The right brain knows the location of the keys. All I need to do is to ask the left hand.

Now when you ask your left hand a question you must be very specific. No mixed messages like, *"Throw the baby down the stairs a cookie."* It will always answer the exact question asked. So I sat at my desk, pen in left hand hovering unsteadily over a plain white sheet of paper, carefully forming my exact question. *"Where ... are ... my ... car ... keys?"*

Well, before my left hand even twitched, I got kind of a hunch, *the glove compartment.* Well, the left-brain, seat of cold logic came unglued, *"Like heck, you say! You didn't put those keys in the glove compartment. I remember ..."* Shut up, left brain! Let right brain answer. *"Where did I put the car keys, right brain?"*

Now, when you do this left-hand writing business, you have to assume that it, the left hand that is servant of the right brain, is something apart from you, a separate entity from the other, so to speak, that has the answer. You have to sit back and wait while it shakes and struggles its way through the forming of letters. *"T h e ... k e y s ... a r e ... "*

At this point my scalp is crawling and I'm feeling tingly because it's so spooky. I'm asking my hand something and it's going to tell me. Think of it! Intrigued, curious, and besides, I got to get going. I say, *"Yes, yes, the keys are?"* And it finishes, *"I n ... t h e ... g l o v e ... c o m ... p a r t ... m e n t."*

"That's so stupid!" Says the left brain.

"Shusssh!" I say. The writing is shaky, but the answer is

the same as the hunch.

My left brain is disgusted. *"No way are the keys in the glove compartment!"*

I have to shusssh the left brain. *"I asked it and it told me and I'm going to look in the glove compartment."*

I walk straight around to the passenger side of the car and find my keys in the lock and remember, *"Oh, yeah! That's were I left 'em."* I'm stoked. This left-hand writing is groovy. My sassy left brain has to remind me it wasn't in the glove compartment. But I'm thinking, *"Picky, picky. So what! It took me on the quickest, easiest route."*

Well, I'm elated about the whole thing. My left brain is still a little grumpy, but doesn't really have a good argument, and my right brain was more than happy to be called on to do the job.

SHY PERSON

Marge was showing me how she would be a shy person. She leaned against the corner, held her elbows close to her sides and quietly looked up and down, her long lashes beautiful and appealing. I thought she did great! I tried it too, in my own way. I stood at a slight incline against the wall to sort of merge with my surroundings. I remained off-center, eyes fixed somewhere mid room.

Marge thought I had my arms too far away from my sides. I was too stiff. I couldn't get it right. Guess I'll always have trouble looking like a shy person, even though I look pretty much like everybody else.

GARDEN WORK

I don't like to work in the yard. Yeah, I know, the ivy needs trimming and branches need pruning and the gravel needs cleaning. You know, the gravel patio? The one where I was going to put the redwood deck someday? Well, it's still the same, and leaves fall from the trees and we hardly see the pretty gravel anymore.

Well, Marge has a way of getting the leaves off. You can't actually sweep the leaves off. Ever try sweeping leaves off a gravel patio? Pretty hard! I tried it once. Said to myself, *"Well, to heck with this!"* Then I slam down my broom and stalk inside where I complain.

Oh, Marge is used to it. My complaining, that is. I get to wash the dishes, instead. Anyway, Marge takes our old Electrolux vacuum cleaner and reverses the attachment end so instead of the vacuum sucking up the leaves, it blows them away. Marge has gotten good at this and is able to blow them all into a nice, neat pile, leaving our pretty gravel patio clean, shiny and new as when I first threw it in there. Sometimes I stop doing dishes and put my head out the sliding patio door and say, *"Whatcha doin' Marge, givin' the patio a blow job? Ha! Ha! Ha! Ha!*

Ha!" I think this is real funny. Then I slam the screen door shut and resume my dishes. Marge doesn't get over this for minutes.

Then there's the ivy that needs trimming. It keeps growing over the sidewalk. I've been goin' to trim that ivy for three years. Marge did half of it one year, but she has a sore arm now and can't physically do it. Well, you can imagine how terrible this makes me feel, her with a sore arm and all. Every week I say to myself, *"Boy, I've got to trim that ivy. It's grown almost all the way across the sidewalk. Another year, it will be growing down the curb and be run over by the cars parking next to our house."* I say to myself, *"You better do something, Roy."*

Well, I'm still going to do it, so I guess I shouldn't feel too bad about myself. And Marge, she doesn't complain much. Just accepts me as I am; a person with good intentions. I'm going to trim those tree branches, too, soon. Last winter, the storm broke off a big one. Nobody was under it, though. That branch, I had to take out. We couldn't even get into the patio with it there. Messed up the gravel patio real bad, too. Marge raked it and gave it a blow job.

Sometimes I think about turning on the sprinklers, too. Especially when the ground cover leaves get brown. Marge usually beats me to it. One day I found a rose blooming quietly, all by itself, in our garden behind the weeds. I made my way through the tangled brush with a pair of pruning shears and cut that old rose right off at the stem and gave it to Marge. She really likes me. I like her, too.

CONNOTATIONS OF BLACK

When helping a favorite client of mine choose a granite countertop for his kitchen counter, I found myself on the subject of colors and their general impact on people. Our discussion was about black, which I know is not a color, but the absence of color. It is in contrast to white, which doesn't seem to be a color though I understand it contains all colors. When black or white is mixed with colors such as yellow, red, blue, green, etc., it strengthens or weakens or muddies or heightens, or lightens or darkens. For me, white and black are the top and bottom of the color chart.

In any case, my client and my sense of reality and definition of beauty were shattered during our visit to the outdoor storage yard of the Empire Marble Company. We saw thousands of tons of stacked, highly polished granite and marble slabs, each as tall as a person and long as a Honda. The variety of colors, shapes and patterns conceived and delivered by Mother Nature was astounding and left us in a state of awe and bewilderment. We settled our nerves, eventually, to look for a good countertop, one both strong and warm, something as a good background for food, yet in harmony with my client's meticulous furniture and well-studied architecture.

Blues, greens, oranges, and reds were too demanding, and we put those out of our thinking. Then we found a slab of black granite overlain with innumerable flecks of tan the size of a man's thumb. This was closer. Some slabs had too much background black showing through, others, less. One slab looked like a starless night overlain with thousands of irregular stars and planets, sometimes separate, sometimes interlocking, but always with too much black demanding to come forth and be seen. What was it about too much or too little black?

I think black gives strength. Mushroom, a white mixed with a sweet beige and black, makes the color purposeful and gives it meaning. Mushroom is stronger than sweet beige because of a little black. Black adds seriousness to sweet tan. Black is no nonsense. Black means business. But too much or too little black got me to thinking about the color, or non-color, black.

Black is the absence of color, the key word being *absence*. Just like a young offspring having no mother or father, black can connote *abandonment*. The void is black, and black is the void. *"He disappeared into the black void!"* Where did he go? We don't know. When we look into blackness we have to ask, *"What's in there?"* Black connotes *mystery*. Sunlight, moonlight and starlight travel through the void's blackness, but anything that's shaded is gone. We can't see anything in the shaded portion. We can guess what's there, but we really don't know what's in there. Black connotes *not knowing*.

At grandmother's house in Chicago, there was a wooden stairway, 30 inches wide, that turned upon itself halfway to the second floor, and at the turning point, where there would normally be a landing, there were pie-shaped stairs. Between the pie-shaped stairs and the second floor there was a cubbyhole with a three-foot-square plywood door painted the same color as the wall. *(Later, we found it led to the attic.)* Even now, the name *cubbyhole* makes me shiver for as kids we were never to look into the cubbyhole. Adults told us the Boogeyman lived there and if we opened the door it would get us. *(The cubbyhole held Christmas presents.)*

One night two of us children turned the painted-to-match latch and swung the door partially open to peer inside. Impenetrable blackness met our vision and we were enveloped by a volume of cold air as if some violent being had just exhaled. We shut and locked it quickly before it could get out, and vowed never to open it again. What was in there? We didn't know. Black connotes *not knowing*.

"When in doubt, paint it out!" Is an architectural rule that means darken it. *"When you're sure, paint it _on_!"* Means lighten it. Darkening means making it closer to black. Small quantities of black can be used as an accent. The letter edged in black is used to announce someone's death. Why black? Because, yellow, red or green is not death-like. The alternatives are not great. Some believe you enter the unconscious realm of blackness when you

die. Black Death! Black symbolizes *death*.

You can accent a picture by outlining lighter portions with a black line. That might be a good thing. This accenting particularly defines that which is outlined. Therefore, black can mean *decisiveness*.

Or, a person who is overweight from the waist down will wear dark trousers or a skirt to minimize or de-emphasize their lower extremities. Whenever attention is not needed, some form of black should be added. Black means *de-emphasized* or *understated*.

And what of the beautiful woman at an exclusive party in a simple black dress, the envy of every woman, and the beauty making every man's heart beat a little faster. Perhaps it's nothing to do with the black dress, but the beautiful woman, for everything de-emphasized, such as the body of a slim woman, accentuates her hands, arms, shoulders, décolleté, hair, make-up and legs. We can see the rest of her looking great, while her black, form-fitting, understated dress minimizes, de-emphasizes and slims her attractive body. Why don't all overweight people wear black? Black is hot in the sun. Perhaps that's the reason.

Black can never be *"the thing,"* because it is in the nature of black to *recede*. White, or red, or yellow, or orange, or green never get lost unless they're in front of similarly colored backgrounds and because it shows up so well, white is always *"the thing!"*

So, the connotations of black are *seriousness, no-nonsense, means-business, absence, abandonment, not knowing, death, decisiveness, de-emphasis, minimization, understatedness* and *slimming.*

But back to choosing a granite slab for the countertops. We chose a slab called *"Blue-Eye."* This slab spoke to my soul because it had the essence of strength and warmth with tiny, evenly spaced, iridescent blue intrusions that added a surprising delicacy and poetic quality. The pattern was mostly of strong flakes of tan covering a black background that added power *(as described above)*, but not so much as to kill or depress the overall statement of the variegated tan flakes. What got to me was the pattern of evenly-spaced bright blue-purple intrusions, a quarter to a half-inch around, that when seen close, was iridescent, but when seen from afar, completely disappeared, leaving the tan, strengthened by the black background, going beautifully and harmoniously with natural wood, food, and the surrounding furniture, accessories and architecture.

CAROB ALMOND CLUSTERS

*M*y daughter sits with her new stepmother beneath a shady tree eating carob-covered almond clusters from a white bag. My new spouse sits delicately on the grass, her arms clasped around her slim knees, exposing well-formed feet in black, strappy Capezios. Reflecting, she replies, *"Perhaps reality is the only place date-sweetened, carob-covered, lightly-toasted almond clusters are to be found, unless, of course, Mrs. Gooch's Natural Foods Market isn't real."*

"Yes," muses my daughter. *"Reality, in this sense, may be more satisfying in heaven."*

At this point, daughter and spouse go into great personal, philosophical and psychological explanations about the meaning of artistic life, one's own place in the divine scheme, the bombastic universe, the value of being well-read and how David Viscott contributes to well-being. They discuss birds, bees, flowers, rain, windstorms, puffy clouds, windswept grasses and the residual power in the trunks of live oaks.

"Did you know Dad used to place the top of his head firmly against the hoary trunk of an ancient oak he found

standing, defended and alone in a vast, grassy valley, resisting gale force winds, in order to sense the adamantine energy, the minute vibrations of the fibrous trunk, the buried grip of its immense foot system, the juxtapositions of power, and the general tenor and attitude of the tree under the powerfully-fluctuating Santa Ana winds?"

The new bride, dressed in a blue, red and white-pocketed skirt, short-sleeved white blouse with open "V" neck and ruffled breast pockets, breathed meaningfully. Her two strands of matching, colored paper beads of similar design, but of somewhat different lengths, lay gracefully about her perfumed neck. Her nude shade *No Nonsense* pantyhose smoothed her shapely calves that terminated in expensive looking, but obtained on sale, shallow blue pumps. Luxurious, gray-stranded hair moved fetchingly on the wind as one clear blue eye narrowed in some inner recognition. *"No, I didn't know he used to do that."*

My blackmailing daughter glanced away to that hard edge where the rounded, spring-green hills meet a powder blue sky, in which patches of voluminous and evenly-spaced gray and white clouds scudded, aloof and subservient toward the hot desert and evaporation. She continued, *"He said, by placing the top of his head in the lee of the wind and against the tree trunk, he could sense the miniscule vibrations of the rough bark, transmitted as if from the tree's spirit. That by listening through the clattering roar of the oak leaves, held firmly by strong stems affixed to dark, fire-scorched branches, he could divine the bearing, disposition and attitude of the tree. He said that though the powerful oak was severely pressured by the relentless gusts, having swept uncontained, along the lean, rolling hills a mile or so through the smooth green valley to stress this tree and any similarly luckless appendages in its relentless path that … "*

"Yes? Yes? What? What?" Cried my colorful consort, arms swinging wildly side-to-side, impatient to end the maddening suspense."

"The tree was not anxious," simply said my daughter.

"The tree was not anxious?" Said M, trying to assess what on God's Holy Earth that meant.

"No!" Said my daughter, twitching her nose a little. *"The ancient oak withstood the pressures of gale-force winds without a hint of anxiety."*

"Mother of Mary, you say!" Cried M, jumping lightly on one foot, awestruck by the magnitude of the revelation.

"Yes!" Said my daughter.

Lovely M flopped back on the silky grass to recover from the concept. They sat beneath the oak absorbing the thought until a cool breeze announced the sun had set.

"Any clusters left?" My gossamer-clad daughter broke the silence.

"Let's split the last one," said Lady M.

MILK BONES

"There, you nasty little doggie! There is your Milk-Bone."

GULP!

"Did you see what that nasty doggie did? Little Hubert? He just gulped that Milk-Bone right down without even chewing it. Now, I'm going to give you another Milk-Bone and this time you chew your food thoroughly. Here's your Milk-Bone."

GULP! GULP!

"Wowie! You doggie! Little Hubert! You nasty doggie! You did it again! You did not chew your food thoroughly. You will have stomach trouble if you do not chew your food thoroughly. Don't look at me with those pleading brown eyes. Daddy says you must chew each bite 32 times to allow for proper digestion. Now, I'm going to give you one more dry Milk-Bone and this time you had better chew it 32 times, or no more bones for you – and to make sure, I'm going to grab your jaws like this and hold them tightly and when I give you this Milk-Bone I'm going to make you chew it 32 times like Daddy says. There!"

GULP! GULP! GULP! WOOF! WOOF!

"OW! You bit me! You nasty little doggie and you only

chewed <u>three</u> times! I'm going to <u>make</u> you chew the other 29 times, just to show you I mean business."

SCUFFLE! SCUFFLE!

"Here! Here! Don't! Don't grab that Milk-Bone box in your mouth! You come back here with that box of doggie Milk-Bones, you nasty doggie — Hubert! Come back here this minute, I say! Come back! Come back! You'll be sorry!"

CINCO DE MAYO

On Friday, Marge had to rent a car. On Saturday, she had to return it. I followed her over to the Thrifty Rent-A-Car and met her at the counter. It cost $33 for one day. On the counter, I noticed a small stack of coupons that said the bearer was entitled to a $25 discount on dinner for two at the Hungry Tiger Country Club Restaurant in Thousand Oaks. It sounded like there might be a catch, but what the ding-dong, Marge had already spent $33 on the car. If we could get a $25 dinner for two, she could almost recoup her losses.

In the afternoon we made reservations, and at 7:30 PM we arrived at the swanky Country Club parking lot. I slipped my Datsun between a Rolls and a Lincoln, and we entered the Hungry Tiger restaurant. I was wearing my two-year-old pale green cords and a white, cotton tennis sweater, the one Lil gave me that she bought for herself, but it was too big. It had a coffee stain on the left wrist and just the tiniest blueberry jam stain on the stomach, just above the belly button and a little to the right when you're looking down.

I figured, whose going to see a couple of little stains? It's dim in those high-class restaurants, anyway. Marge looked great as always. She's a high-stepper. We were greeted by the hostess and two managers. The restaurant was almost full. Through the latticework we could see tanned, beautiful people laughing, talking, eating salad and sipping green drinks. The manager was pleasantly surprised to see we had a reservation. I could tell we looked like *somebody* in his eyes by the way he said, *"Right this way."*

We moved gracefully between the chairs and tables. I didn't bump into any tables or knock a butter knife onto somebody's lap or anything. Presently, we were seated at a very nice table with a clean linen tablecloth. It was near a picture window with a splendid view of the golf course set among hazy ridges of lavender mountains. Through the tinted glass, the twilight colors were exceptionally rich.

Soon our waitress asked if we were ready to order. I decided to be forthright with her and told her we were here for the Thrifty Rent-A-Car coupon dinner. The smile faded ever so slightly as she folded up the real menu and said the coupon dinner had a selection of only four items, lobster, of which, was not one. I ordered scallops and Marge ordered shrimp. By way of being humorous, I told the waitress, *"We are your basic coupon customers. Ha! Ha! Ha!"*

She asked, *"House dressing, or bleu cheese?"*

Marge and I both got *"House."*

One of the best parts of the coupon dinner was the huge glass of Chablis given us before the meal. In no time we were having the time of our lives, talking, laughing and eating. I told Marge, *"Hey, Marge! We could go back to Thrifty Rent-A-Car and pick us up a couple more coupons and eat at a couple of other Hungry Tiger restaurants."*

Well, the meal was just great. I jokingly mentioned, *"We'll get 10 feet outside the restaurant and be arrested for larceny by some plainclothesman."* On leaving, I insisted on telling the two managers and the hostess how much I appreciated the coupon dinner and how terrific I thought Thrifty Rent-A-Car was. We said goodbye and walked to our car at the far end of the lot.

Well, you know, it seemed things were going just too good. Glancing around, I see this manager come running out of the restaurant with a paper in his hand. I say to Marge, *"Oh! Oh! Here it comes!"* In a trice the man is in front of us and out of breath, but still dignified. He explains there has been a misunderstanding and that the coupon really means they are giving us a $32 dinner, charging us only $25 for using Thrifty Rent-A-Car. We save $7, but owe him 25 bucks.

I knew there was a catch to it. Dad used to say, *"There's no such thing as a free lunch."* That goes for dinners, too. I hauled out my wallet intending to go *"plastic."* The manager said he was sorry and we told them we would walk him back to the cashier's stand so he could write up the ticket. We did and not too many of the people looked up. Guess most of them didn't know what had happened.

On the way out we looked in the bar. A live combo was

setting up for the evening's musical program. We decided to sit down and listen to a couple of sets. The cocktail waitress came to take our orders. I slumped back in my chair, showed my sweatered stomach and said, *"I couldn't eat another thing."*

Soon we were dancing to the rock-and-roll band and having a great time. The female vocalist asked if there were any *"occasions"* to celebrate that anyone could think of. No one in the room answered. I thought for a moment, then called out, *"CINCO DE MAYO."* Which, in fact, it was. The vocalist said, *"Oh, yeah!"* then played a catchy little Mexican tune. We left about 11:00 PM.

LET'S BE HOT!

Hot! I can think big thoughts. Like, universe! That's big. *"The universe is big!"* How about <u>that</u> for a big thought. Or spirituality! That's vague. See? I can be vague and big! Try this one on for size. What is God? There's a question for you. You think you know the answer? I've been trying to get that one for years and they're still not agreeing.

Like Shiva and Shakti had something to do with gods. Over in the islands near Japan, I think. I don't know everything. That's a mark of intelligence, you know. If you can say, *"I Don't Know Everything!"* that means you're smart. Or Buddha is sort of God-like. And take Hinduism. That's a big subject. In fact all religions are a big subject. Maybe too big to go into right now.

Consider philosophy. Take Nietzche, for instance. He was a philosopher, as was Kant. Those philosophers brought up a lot of subjects, like war and peace. In fact, one writer wrote about that. I think it was Tolstoy. Take George Bernard Shaw, for instance. He was a vegetarian. Go ahead, check it out! He was! Carlos Castaneda was borderline. But, he had some cogent things to say. Cogent, cogent, cogent! Cogent means deep!

So, I have talked about the universe, religion and philosophy so far. I'm hot! These are very big subjects, but my knowledge doesn't stop there. How about mathematics? I know about Einstein, who deduced that $E=mc^2$. How many people could do that? Not everybody, I'll tell you. Maybe, even nobody. Maybe, even, Einstein was the only one.

Or the great computer mathematicians that thought up this intricate system of chips and globules of wires and parts garbled together so I can use this wonderful word processing machine to type with. Brilliant! I say, Brilliant!

And musicians are wonderful people, too. Like, I just heard Beethoven's Violin Concert in D major or D minor or D-flat major, or D-sharp minor or D-flat minor, or D-sharp major, played by Mehta and Zuckerman. One of those. And music is mathematical, because when you're singing, you have to count to stay on the beat, and music is written in numbers like four beats or three beats to the measure, and there are sixteenth notes, one note, half note, no note, a whole note. Very mathematical.

Even division comes in to play, since a bar is divided into equal parts divisible by the number <u>one</u>. And multiplication comes into play according to the sheets you have to hand out in relation to the people to receive them. Like, 30 singers need 30 scores, 1 x thirty, "I Like that."

So, I'm hot! Though I'll give you your due. If you can follow this, you must be somewhat hot yourself. It takes one to know one. Let's be hot!

BRAIN NEWS

The Brain is Like a Cassette Deck

The head is like a cassette deck. The brain is a tape, but sometimes the power is off. Some brains are old and need rewinding while others sometimes get stuck on fast-forward. Some have two programs hidden on one tape, both going at the same time. Thoughtless people may have unintentionally hit the pause button. Many people are on full erase, but then, sometimes the heads need cleaning. Unfortunately, you can't get a new one, but sometimes a cold shower helps.

Brain News

At the Museum of Science and Industry, they have an electrical machine that tests the amount of current you can stand passing through your brain.

You stand in a pan of water and bite on a soft metal-plated bar while turning a dial on a thermostat calibrated from 1 to 10.

The new theory is that the more electricity your brain can stand, the smarter you are.

People have scored as high as 8.5 or 9.0 before passing out.

Some tried to show they were brilliant and were sped to the hospital.

Others turned the dial right up to 10 and felt nothing.

Controversy has arisen over the machine's safety and usefulness; however, museum officials have found the machine to be perfectly safe, if not very useful.

The Brain is Like a Washing Machine

Psychology Today reports the normal brain is like a washing machine that all day long goes *wishy-washy, wishy-washy.* But they say if a person has too much coffee, the brain can buzz, whirl and hum like the spin cycle, and if a cigarette or two is added it can get overloaded and start the death-wobbles, going *Blunk! Blum! Zonk! Bam!* much like washing gym shoes with no towels. They recommend quitting cigarettes and decreasing coffee too, so you can again enjoy your brain just going *wishy-washy, wishy-washy.*

WHAT TO WEAR TO THE CONCERT

I don't have anything to wear to the Music Center.

You'll think of something. I'm wearing my new royal purple dress.

You don't care what I wear, do you?

I love you.

I could wear my pastel green cords and my turtleneck sweater?

Hmmm!

It's too hot and scratchy, though. How about a tan sweater with patches on the elbows? I could smoke a pipe and go as a writer.

Very funny.

I think I'll wear my socks without the holes. I'll feel better even though the colors don't match.

Your socks don't match?

They're pretty close and they're clean. I haven't worn them since the black tie wedding.

My God!

I only have one pair of decent shoes, you know. The brown loafers. I could shine them up real good, except I don't think they'd go with the green cords. And the sizes are wrong.

What do you mean?

The right shoe is eight and a half and the left is nine.

You could kick one off under the seat when you get there.

Yeah! It's dark, anyway. Are you sure you won't be embarrassed to be seen with me?

You can go any way you like.

What if I went in my *"Mickey Rat"* T-shirt and *"Norbert Nerd"* hat?

Nobody would watch the concert. I wouldn't worry about what to wear. This is Southern California. People attend concerts like these in all sorts of dress.

How about I go in my helmet and goggles? I could get a white scarf for my neck and go as Cary Grant, British war ace.

That should knock 'em dead.

Or I could wear my nose and glasses and white sneakers with no socks and go as Woody Allen.

How about going as yourself? It's only a concert.

Who's conducting, anyway?

Giuliani, with Alfred Brindel as the concert pianist.

I still don't know what to wear.

Why don't you wear a tux?

What? Spend forty-five dollars for one evening? Who am I trying to impress? I don't know anyone there!

Then why are you worried about what to wear? Go in your work clothes. No one's going to notice, anyway.

I need a haircut, too.

You look all right. Maybe a little trim ...

See how this hair sticks straight out above my ears? I feel ratty! Just ratty! That's the only word for it.

How about buying an outfit?

By Thursday? It's only Tuesday! They wouldn't have time to do the alterations. Besides, I hate to be rushed when I pick out an important outfit.

Oh? When was the last time you picked out an important outfit?

The fall of '79, I think, or was it '78? It's not something you do every day, you know.

How about borrowing some clothes, then?

Who do I know that's my size? Anyway, it's presumptuous borrowing clothes, don't you think? I wish you hadn't thrown out my suits Joe gave me.

They didn't fit.

They cost Joe Waters four hundred dollars each. You threw out sixteen hundred dollars worth of suits.

I didn't throw them out. We gave them to Goodwill.

I didn't even get credit on my tax return for deductible gifts.

Why not?

I forgot to retain the receipt.

I thought you said I threw out ...

Well, I actually took them down there, but you made me do it.

They didn't fit you. They belonged to Joe Waters!

So they were a little heel-worn at the cuffs.

And shiny on the rump.

I think I looked like Humphrey Bogart in the pinstriped one, didn't you?

You were magnificent.

And the coat sleeves were a little long ... just showed my fingertips. The collars were large, too ... used to set back off my neck about two inches ... gave me a powerful upper body look.

You looked ridiculous in those suits. They weren't your style at all.

I thought my flashy tie took your mind off the suit.

The flowered one? Come on, now.

I used to wear those suits with my shirt with the cut-off sleeves at the elbow. I looked pretty sharp, as long as I didn't have to take off my coat.

What are you going to wear to the concert?

Sigh! I don't know. How about my white cotton sweater ... no, it's got coffee stains.

How about that sweater I gave you?

It's got a ruffly waist. What would I wear with it, a tie? I could pretend I took off my suit-coat because it was too hot.

You'll think of something by Thursday.

Yeah.

CONNOTATIONS OF WHITE

*F*irst there was void and darkness. I don't know who made void and darkness, but I presume it was also God who made it before he could say, *"Let there be light!"* Scientists say light was introduced at the time of the big bang and continues through all the stars we can see and through our sun. I am glad to report on planet earth our sun is the source of light. And I have to ask myself what is its color? The answer is light is white. There is nothing whiter than the white of the big bang or the sun. God might also have said, *"Let his beings see light,"* for that seems to me as great a miracle. Of course you have to have been made a creature before He could give the gift of light and sight and white. Of God's creations, I am one, and I thank my lucky stars *(or thank God, as the case may be, since he made the stars, too)*, for this supreme gift. God also gave me a brain and the inspiration and limited ability to discuss the connotations of white.

The white sun is the exact opposite of the space through which it travels, impenetrable black. White is *up* and black is down. White is *on* and black is off. White is *right* and black is wrong. Who ever heard of Snow Black and the

Seven Dwarfs? It's Billie Burke, the good Snow <u>White</u>, or Margaret Hamilton, the Wicked Witch of the West, always dressed in black, who rides a broom and cackles, while the good witch, Burke, wears a tiara, carries a wand, and is clothed in a white party dress. Could the white witch do anything wrong? No! Could the black Wicked Witch of the West do anything wrong? You bet! That's her job. White equals *right*. Black equals *wrong*.

I was looking at the stars last night twinkling in the impossible distance, and imagined one of them as my home. I began to long to go back through those impossible distances to my home; to my beautiful blue planet, far away, revolving around my beautiful white star, the sun, accompanied by the magic brilliance of a moon that whirled and changed sizes; full moon, half moon, then getting lost for a few days and surprising me some early evening as a delicate crescent.

I thought to myself, *"What am I doing so far away from my home, twirling around in this limitless space?"* It was outlandish that I was so far away, living on this big, round, foreign rock that was attached to nothing at all, circling a different sun with no means of support. The planet and I are held up in outer space by no-see-ums: gravity, magnetism, the impossible forces of dark matter and dark energy. *(I can't get off.)*

But what does this have to do with connotations of the color white? Nothing, except stars, mostly suns, send bright, white colors through a black void for hundreds and thousands of light years, reaching our eyes from inconceivable distances. The stars also send colors from great distances including white that is connected with the Great Unknowable, God, and contains all colors. White is a color that can be seen from a distance better than any other. Connotations: White is *archetypal* and *God-like*, the exact opposite of the black void.

Philosophically, *God = light = white = seeing = brain = consciousness.* And also, God = dark = no light = no sight = no comprehension = no brain = unconsciousness. Therefore white equals *consciousness*. Black equals unconsciousness. Isn't that simple?

White is pure, such as, *"pure as the driven snow",* snow being white, and all. The Prince on the white horse is the desired Prince because having the white horse and having no black on him, we think him *pure, gentle, courageous, protective, strong. (White horses are strong and productive.)* Chivalrous knights are always desirable and always on a white horse. They're attractive and we men and women like them.

When a fast rain leaves high mist in the setting sun, it creates an arching rainbow that sometimes encircles a green mountain. It has all colors except black.

Or turn a CD at a special angle to the sun and ribbons of rainbow are reflected to the eye. With a DVD player we hear sound and see colors as vibrations.

In the near-death experience, some see a white light at the end of a tunnel. It's not red, or blue, or black, or yellow. It's white. White means something *good* is going to happen.

White can be seen more than any other color. When things are lighter we notice them better. It would be good if the nicer things to see were lighter and the things we don't want to see are darker. If you like it, show it. If you're in doubt, paint it out.

So white connotes *God who made it, creatures who can see it, impossible distances, up (not down), on (not off), right, (not wrong), consciousness, (not unconsciousness) learning, purity, power, importance, and desirability and no doubt many more positive things.* Aren't we lucky?

MIND TRAVELER

*H*aving glanced at the Old Testament lately, I noticed brilliant stories were usually told with the predominant use of the word, *"and"* such as, *"<u>And it came to pass</u>, ..."* or, *"<u>And they gathered together</u>..."* or, *"<u>And thus spake Samuel,</u>"* etc., etc., and I thought since it seemed a tried-and-true method of telling a story, I'd take a chance connecting thought to thought with the word *"and,"* and see how it goes.

And so it <u>came</u> to pass ... *(Did I plagiarize? Gulp!)* And it <u>went</u> to pass... No! ... And in the beginning, there was a ten-year-old boy named David who lived on the edge of a quiet lake to the north of a big city (that boomed and purred like a cat on your lap) *(I know this is an indulgent phrase not advancing the story line, but I like it anyway, and I thought I'd share it with you.)* and he lived with his Mother and Dad and his sixteen-year-old sister, Anna. And the boy loved the peaceful nature of the lake that steamed in the coolness of the morning and froze in the cold of a windswept winter, and it was trees, leaves, rainstorms and flowers that also thus spake to him of contentment.

And David did attend the eighth grade at Barnsdall

middle school, and Anna was a sophomore at Middleton High, and as I get deeper into this story, I don't think I want to get David into <u>too</u> much trouble, though if I don't get him in <u>some</u> kind of trouble, there won't be much of a story, so I must invent a problem in which he is involved without completely destroying his psyche while still teaching him something worthwhile. And thus it shall come to pass that Anna, if she does anything at all, will be a <u>supportive</u> character and this feels good to me, since I dislike stories with serious troubles and can't abide getting either David or Anna into any <u>real</u> trouble and, let's face it, my own character is such that I only like to think happy thoughts and far be it from me to take you, my readers, if any, through a serious problem, since we have enough of that watching the news on TV.

And so it came to pass *(there I go again)*, that David's peculiar characteristic was that he could do mind travel, and so it looks like we have a story about a ten-year-old boy who can travel in his mind and his adventures could take him wherever his mind *(my mind)* takes him and so I'll make it that it was Saturday and he was free to arise early for a rowboat ride for pleasure into the lake and at the crack of dawn. There was the customary fog of early morning, but he wasn't discouraged, and so he arrived barefoot at the pier with T-shirt and jeans and lightly stepped on boards that shook slightly with his footfall, sending ripples in ever-widening circles disappearing into the dim and foggy waters.

And so David stepped gently into the boat and seated himself on the rear wooden seat and taking one oar out of its socket, pushed himself into the early morning fog and he began rowing close to shore to keep his bearings. And he observed the surprisingly green lily pads reflecting in the dim light, their stems descending into the cool, clear water where they were eventually lost to view in the watery depths, while now and then a frog escaping the commotion pushed downward with thrusting legs as David's oars made regular glipp-lipp sounds. And it was his intent to approach a shallow river outlet farther down the shore following along a mysterious grove of young willow trees, their trunks partially submerged, barely seen through the fog that were standing silent, dim and motionless, on the shoreline.

But, as luck would have it, the intensity of the fog increased and though he strained his eyes he soon could no longer see the shore, and could detect nothing beyond the boat, the oars, and the quietly racing water close to the gunwales. Yet he moved forward purposefully, hoping the fog would clear, when suddenly, the oars voluntarily lifted from the water, sending droplets onto the silky-smooth surface of the water and then the entire rowboat and David magically arose, dripping from water into misty air.

David was astounded and fearful at his apparent loss of control as the oars shipped themselves and though he wished the rowboat to return to the water so he could continue his early morning adventure, his wishes were in vain when he discovered it was not going to happen. And the rowboat continued ascending, whether he liked it or not and he held to the seat and sides of the boat in tense apprehension and then the boat and David broke through the top of the cottony surface of the fog revealing billowing tops of fog-clouds that soon lay well below him as he and his rowboat continued rising into the air at increasing speed.

As the charmed rowboat with hapless David rose into the sky, the morning sun, its face big and stern, was suspended in the east, low above the trees, glaring with purposeful intention and David looked down over the side of the boat and the ground was moving fast and he saw square, trapezoidal and triangular patches of land in yellows, reds, greens and browns that were fields of corn, cabbage, tomatoes and oats. And he and the boat rose so high, he was astonished to make out what seemed like the whole state of Texas, including the panhandle and as he sped southward ever higher, he made out the drifting deserts and eroded mountaintops of Mexico, while immediately below him was the blue Gulf of California and to the West, the slim, rocky backbone of Baja. And then he was lifted even higher into the atmosphere over the beautiful, blue Pacific and as he shot along the Central American coast, he saw the finely-etched shores of Guatemala, Honduras and San Salvador and at the equator, the heat was building and the bewitched rowboat with its astounded passenger sailed over Nicaragua, Costa Rica and Panama, where his sharp eyes could make out the slim, man made waterways with the lake in-between that linked the Atlantic to the Pacific. And farther to the east over the Caribbean, from his great height, he spied an immense spiral-shaped cloud that was a rapidly building hurricane with a menacing eye whirling dead center and clearly visible.

And he accelerated past the equator, ascending to ever-higher altitudes over the slender, sinuous mountain range lacing Columbia, Ecuador and Peru, where powerful mountains were rigidly held in long, jagged, ice-formed shapes that stretched as far as the eye could see. And upward he traveled through Chile and high over the snow-covered plains of Patagonia.

Frighteningly cold, he crossed the South Pole, but his rowboat, under a spell, paid no attention as they moved into the darker sky that was a bluish shade of black and he could see the curvature of the earth as he flashed over the Pole, rounded the bottom of the world, and up and over the other side, catching glimpses of New Zealand, Australia, Japan, Russia and then over the North Pole, where he was slung at a terrifying speed into outer space on a trajectory toward the Moon.

(I've gotten David into quite a little fix now, haven't I? Where will he go? How will I end it?)

David has been slingshotted out of this world, heading for the moon. Within eight minutes, he reached the moon, swooping one time around, trying to see the blackened backside, but saw nothing because it was in impossible shade and then the moon's gravity whipped him farther into a spatial path to the red planet of Mars and that took him the better part of a half-hour, but the experience was so intense that time was of no interest, nor had he anything to say about it because the charmed boat had decided to actually land on Mars.

And so it came thusly to pass, *again*, that the boat landed David on a broad, flat, red, stony plain, with jagged, other-planetary mountains erratically leaping about, the wind blowing insanely and the red planet's reflections giving the boat and David a ruddy complexion. And David couldn't leave the boat for fear it might leave without him and he gazed upward into cold, black space and among the multitudinous stars that blew like a fog before him, he saw a small, blue, spherical and wondrous object glowing steadily and distinctly with a white moon circling like a pearl and he thought it stunning and he loved it, because he knew it to be his home and longed to be on earth and smell his mom's pork chops and see his sister, Anna and eat a dish of cool, canned pears, when just that quickly the boat lifted at harrowing speed, leaving David momentarily flattened against his rowboat seat.

And the God-powered rowboat launched itself, spinning through black space past Saturn, Uranus, Jupiter and then past that forlorn little ice glob, Pluto and streaked toward the Large and Small Magellanic Clouds, both billion-star galaxies, bound by gravity to each other and to the Milky

Way, where the boat circled once and then raced off to the splattered remains of an enormous cosmic explosion resulting in the Crab Nebula that he and the boat circled twice. And then to examine a strange, dim, light that looked like a star, but was really a faraway galaxy with a scientific number, but called a Quasar, and they circled that three times and then toward a force so powerful that even light cannot escape it – a black hole.

David was terrified when the boat became locked into the event horizon, that *"...one-way surface that once penetrated, the laws of gravity ensure there is no turning back, no escaping the powerful gravitational grip." (From Brian Greene's book, The Elegant Universe)* And his knuckles were white holding tightly to the seat with blond hair flying and the boat descended into an ever-tightening spiral *(like a bug going down a drain)*, toward that ominous black circle in the middle. And once there in the pitch-blackness, he involuntarily rolled his eyes upward to say a simple prayer, *"Now I lay me down to sleep, etc.,"* as he and the boat were compressed into less than the size of a pinpoint and then, when they were so tiny that an atom looked as big as a house, they suddenly exploded out the other side, still squeezed into a tiny, one-dimensional filament, sailing through the universe faster than the speed of light at trillions of miles per second, through infinite numbers of wraps and warps and ripples and wriggles, through galaxies and gasses, implosions, explosions, quasars and pulsars, multicolored clouds in crowds, etc. And then, by way of the string theory, through an infinitely long tube-like space that wound itself around like a Gordian Knot, left, right, up, down, sideways, backwards, upside down, right-side up, inverted, extraverted, imploded, exploded, inside-out and reassembled, broken and resurrected, as he and the boat ratcheted through several of eleven other dimensions. And David squelched an urge to barf his cookies before the magic boat flew, twisting and spiraling, out the other end to fly around more of the astounding universe on the other side of the black hole.

(Well this is all very well and good, but now that he's been on the other side of a black hole in a different universe and has gone through other dimensions, what else can happen to him and how can I get him home? To finish or not to finish, that is the question.)

And for a while David experienced the dim, mental haze like someone who was just coming out of a stroke, until his eyes slowed their rotating and he saw an entire symphonic orchestra playing the brilliant scherzo near the end of Beethoven's Ninth while at the same time recalling his school instructors words, *"Only 4% of the universe can be seen and detected and the other 96% necessary to keep the universe running is in the form of dark matter and dark energy, both of which are invisible and undetectable."* And then it was revealed to his soul that God lay in the realm of dark matter and energy. How else could the whole universe keep running? How personal! How impersonal! How brilliant! How beyond comprehension!

Relentless, the magic rowboat took David on an extended tour of the other universe, in fact, lots of other universes that we suspect blew his mind and he discovered more things in other universes than he knew about his own universe. I won't mention them here because how am I supposed to know what's in another universe on the other side of a black hole while operating under the influences of string-theory?

But one thing he did <u>not</u> know was that each of the millions and billions of galaxies had its own black hole located approximately in the center and he did <u>not</u> know that the magic boat, being enchanted and all, knew which black hole of all the millions and billions, could send him on a journey back to his own universe and ultimately home.

And he found that within a few degrees from the spectacular Orion Nebula is the Horsehead Nebula *(nebula means galaxy and the dark shape that resembles a horsehead is a huge gaseous cloud that blocks the vision of billions of stars behind)*, and at a short distance *(five or six light years)* from the tip of the dark cloud resembling a horse's head is a black hole and the boat confidently entered this black hole's event horizon, that circular plane where anything affected, like the boat and David, could never escape or even be seen again, and David and his boat began their swirling, drainpipe-like ride down toward that infinitely small black hole, and once entering were almost immediately blasted into a more welcome outer space containing millions and billions of stars, but particularly one beautiful blue planet with a circling, pearl-like moon called Earth.

Skimming along the treetops, the rowboat flew swiftly to David's lake, circled once, and landed with a shoosh and a splash in the now-clear water, the fog having lifted in the early afternoon and the frog, once again, sunning himself on the lily pad and the boat having relinquished its powers, David rowed home and when asked by his sister, Anna, *(the single supporting member of the cast)* "How was your morning?"

David answered, *"Fine."*

TUXEDO

*Y*esterday I was invited to a *black tie* wedding. Right away, that sounds ominous. *Black tie* sounds more like a funeral. I didn't want to ask what a *black tie* wedding was, so I look my friend and his fiancée in the eye, real straight, like I know what they mean. I figure I'll ask somebody later what it means.

Then later, I ask my friend, Jim, and he says *tuxedo*, that's what it means. White shirt, black tie and *tuxedo*. There's no way out of it. And my Marge, she have to wear a *gown*, because the men come in *black tie* and the ladies come in *gowns*.

Well, I don't own a suit or even a sport coat let alone a black tie tuxedo. I ask Jim what I'm supposed to do. He says, well, he got a coupla old ones hangin' in the closet since '92. There's a bit o' dust on the top of the shoulders, but we could pat it off. I look at Jim. He's big and I'm short. I figure the pants are goin' to be too long. I figure, maybe we could roll 'em up, not so far's to show my argyles.

"No argyles!" Says Jim.

We discuss renting a tuxedo and how much that costs these days. They ain't cheap is the upshot, I explain to Jim.

Maybe I better buy something I could use later so I don't waste that *"rent"* money, like maybe a brown corduroy sport coat with patches on the elbows. I could borrow a pipe and go as an author.

Jim says, *"Nope!"* I better rent a tuxedo. I say, Marge has to wear a gown. I could get her a bolt of corduroy and she could make a gown and we could go matched. Jim didn't think much of the idea, but, you see, I'm terrified. I know whatever I wear I'm going to look like a clown.

The man at the gate will say, *"Show people use the rear door!"* He liable to ask, *"Where's your red nose and plastic chicken?"* Then laugh.

I just know I'm goin' to look weird, but what're you goin' to do?

BLUE GRASS
RED TREES
SPRING BREEZE
CLEAN GLASS
WRINKLED KNEES
QUIET SNEEZE
LARGE FEES
YELLOW BEES
GOLF TEES
AND GALAXIES
WILL SOON PASS.

AFTERWORD

I enjoyed thinking about these essays and stories and wanted them to be properly protected between two strong covers for private reference. In that way the book is harder to throw away, assuring me of a slightly longer mortality *(Or continued harassment as the case may be)*. Later on, if anyone reads them at all, the state of my mind will be resoundingly clear, won't it? Thank you for reading.

Doug

ACKNOWLEDGEMENTS

I give thanks to my beautiful wife, Marge, who has listened graciously to all the readings and has generously donated her objective viewpoints and considered opinions. I wish to thank Helane Freeman without whose passion and hard work designing and publishing this book would not have been possible. I wish to thank my good friend, Ron Munro, who introduced me to Wordstar and subsequent computers many years ago and who has generously supported my efforts ever since. I appreciate my friend and son-in-law, Tom Rincker, owner of Applications Recording and computer expert, a person I've become particularly dependent upon for continuing moral support and computer advice. Thanks to any and all readers, everyone mentioned in my stories, my loving family, Huey, the one-eyed neighbor dog and my office plant getting much too large for its corner.

Isn't it miraculous this special group is all together at this pinpoint in geologic time on this rare planet with its own sun and moon and all of us sailing through space as dignified members of our own personal galaxy orbiting its own black hole? Thanks to all!   *Doug Rucker*

A BRIEF BIOGRAPHY

After finishing the eighth grade in Chicago, Illinois, Doug was awarded a scholarship to the Chicago Art Institute. He entered Austin High School, won five letters in three major sports, and took a three-year college preparatory course in architecture. At the University of Illinois in Champaign-Urbana he was awarded a Bachelor of Science degree and afterward worked as a draftsman in Denver, San Diego and Pasadena. In Altadena he married drama and art graduate, Karon Conan, and received his California license to practice architecture. Continuing drafting in Glendale and later in Brentwood he moved into a house of his own design in Santa Monica Canyon where Karon gave birth to three marvelous daughters. In 1958 he opened his own office in Malibu and built his own Malibu *"dream house"* overlooking Surfrider Beach. The forty-two-foot-square

main floor floated on a pedestal thirty-five feet in the air with a wrap-around deck and spectacular views of the Malibu Creek estuary, the Movie Colony, Surfrider Beach and Serra Retreat.　He received much newspaper and magazine notoriety before a brush fire late in 1970 burned it to the ground. By the end of 1972 he'd built an entirely different, more fire resistant and equally dramatic house over the same foundations. It was similarly honored and published, but lost to a divorce in 1980. Later the same house was listed with his peers, Frank Lloyd Wright, Richard Neutra, Frank　Ghery, John Lautner, etc., in the Guide to Architecture in Los Angeles. He is proud of his 54 year vocation as an architect doing small homes and remodeling in Malibu.　Until retirement six years ago, architecture has been the first and foremost focus of his life. Doug and Marge, his wife of almost 30 years, are enjoying the creative life in a very small house on an acre of land in the mountains a few miles above Malibu. For the past six years he's been enjoying writing books and showing his reflection and abstract photography in local galleries.

www.ingramcontent.com/pod-product-compliance
Lightning Source LLC
Chambersburg PA
CBHW071951260326
41914CB00004B/794